BOOK VI
THE
TRUCKING
PIONEERS
by
Mike K. Terebecki

Pioneer Press
4338 Dover Crossing Drive
Marietta, GA 30066
(770) 591-7300

First Edition   ©1996
by   Pioneer Press
    4338 Dover Crossing Drive
    Marietta, GA 30066

Additional copies of Books II, III, IV, V and VI may be ordered from :

Pioneer Press
4338 Dover Crossing Drive
Marietta, GA 30066
(770) 591-7300
    or
American Truck Historical Society
P.O. Box 531168
Birmingham, AL 35259

DISCLAIMER

Much of the historical information included in this book was supplied to the author by the companies themselves. Over 35 years of collecting trucking facts and memorabilia has gone into the preparation of this book.

The main purpose of this book is a remembrance of the trucking pioneers for their contribution to the industry.

Every attempt has been made to verify pertinent historical facts, but this was not always possible.

Neither the author nor the publisher accepts any responsibility for the accuracy of the historical content.

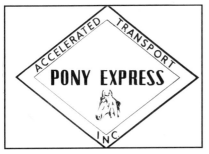

ACCELERATED TRANSPORT - PONY EXPRESS, INCORPORATED HAGERSTOWN, MD

It all started when Harry G. Masser was offered a job at Armour and Company by his father-in-law. While working as a shipping clerk for the company, Harry became interested in starting a trucking company. Harry resigned from his job and bought a second-hand one ton truck. On July 4, 1931, he started Masser Motor Express and made $96.00 profit the first week. (Armour and Company was one of Harry's first customers.)

With a lot of hard work, the company began to grow. Harry's wife, Pearl, was very supportive and helped him in any way she could. Routes were established from Hagerstown, MD to New York, NY; Philadelphia, PA; Baltimore, MD; and Washington, DC.

Around 1940, Harry bought Baggerly Express of Winchester, VA and opened a terminal there. In 1942, Harry bought Kite Transfer of Charles Town, WV. This purchase extended routes into West Virginia and the western part of Virginia.

Early equipment included Chevrolets, Internationals, Diamond-T's, Fords, and Whites. Most of the company owned trucks were painted blue with red and silver lettering. The company also started to use lease operators in the late 1940's.

Around 1950, J. Edward Davey joined the company as a 50% owner. In return for his partnership, Mr. Davey was to help the company financially and to gain control of Cumberland Motor Express and merge the two companies. Shortly after Davey joined the company, the name was changed from Masser Motor Express to Accelerated Transport Pony Express, Inc. Now the company trucks were painted green and, unlike before, the lease operators were forced to paint their trucks the uniform green color as well.

By the mid-1950's, Pony Express operated approximately 300 units with an annual income of around $2,500,000. They operated 13 terminals in four states including NJ, PA, WV, and MD. For a short period of time, terminals were also operated in Charles Town, WV; Cumberland, MD; and Winchester, VA.

Pony Express was one of the few truck lines to offer direct service from points in West Virginia to New York, NY, Philadelphia, PA and Baltimore, MD. Because of this fact, Pony Express had more freight coming out of West Virginia than they could handle, making it difficult for the company to keep their trucks loaded going into West Virginia.

Most of the company's road tractors were supplied by owner operators in the late 1950's and early 1960's. A lot of these owner operators used B model and H model Macks. As of 1962, Pony Express leased a total of 96 tractors. The company owned road tractors were supplied by White and straight trucks were supplied by Ford. Fruehauf supplied Pony Express with vans, open tops, flat beds, and reefers to haul their freight.

Pony Express operated up until 1965 when it was sold to Hall's Motor Transit Company. Harry Masser continued to work in the trucking industry, after his company was sold, as an organizer of the Western Maryland Trucking Association and on the board of advisors for the pension fund of the Hagerstown Teamsters Union. He was also a member of the American Truck Historical Society. Unfortunately, Harry G. Masser died on January 23, 1991 at the age of 84.

Note: D. L. George and Sons of Hagerstown, MD and Waynesboro, PA currently operates its fine looking fleet as "Accelerated Pony Express."

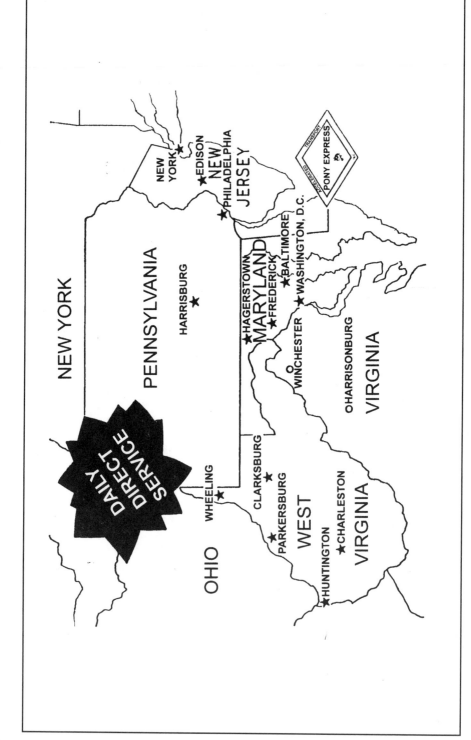

"We Do It Right The First Time"

BENTON EXPRESS, INC.
ATLANTA, GA

Brothers B.D. and Lex Benton were both foremen for the Western Electric Company. They were both laid off during the depression that followed the crash of 1929. Pooling their savings, they rented an old service station. (The deal also included a two bedroom house, a barbeque stand, and an old Ford panel truck.)

In those days, most movie film was transported by Railway Express, with one of the film runs being from the Atlanta depot to Birmingham, AL. When one of the film drivers began trading with the Benton Brothers Service Station, the brothers first learned about the film distribution business. At the time, no film was being transported from Atlanta into south Georgia by truck. Theater owners had to pick up their film at the nearest railroad station.

In 1934, the brothers put their used panel truck to use by providing film delivery and pick up service to south Georgia. Soon their service spread all over south Georgia and by 1941, extended into Jacksonville, FL. When the union struck Railway Express in 1948, the film companies asked Benton Brothers to deliver to the entire state of Florida, and they did.

The company continued to grow by expanding its

capabilities for delivering time-sensitive materials such as film, newspapers, magazines, and express air freight. No acquisitions have taken place during the long history of Benton Express.

In 1959, Lex Benton bought out his brother and gradually moved the company into general freight hauling. Eventually, the company name was changed to Benton Express, Inc. When Lex Benton passed away in 1973, Herb Matthews (a veteran of 15 years with the company) took over as president. The company was grossing about $1.75 million at the time.

After the Motor Carriers Act of 1980 which deregulated interstate transportation of freight, Benton Express was in an excellent position to expand its general commodities business while many other carriers closed down or were fighting to survive. More equipment was purchased and terminals were added in GA, FL, AL, the Carolinas, and most recently in TN.

Benton Express, over the years, has used a wide variety of equipment including Chevrolet P & D units to road tractors supplied by GMC, KW, White, IH and a score of R model Macks purchased in 1984 and 1985. (One of these R models now boasts 1.6 million miles of nearly 24 hour-a-day running on its original engine.) The company policy of buying good used equipment may be changing with the recent acquisition of bright new IH and Volvo/White road tractors.

About 90% of the company's freight is next day, with the other 10% being 2nd day delivery. With the company's extensive experience in delivering time-sensitive material, Benton Express is proud of its 98.4% on-time delivery record.

Herb Matthews, who was named president of the Georgia Motor Trucking Association, has guided Benton Express from a small film distributor into a major southeastern carrier with revenues in excess of $30 million. The company utilizes 300 tractors, 700 trailers, and 60 trucks out of their 21 company owned terminals. Film delivery remains 3% of total company business.

Raleigh

Charlotte

Greenville

Rome   Athens

Atlanta

Augusta

Charleston

Columbus   Dublin

Savannah

Moultrie

Pensacola

Tallahassee

Jacksonville

Ocala

Orlando

Tampa

West Palm
Beach

Fort Myers

Miami

BILKAYS EXPRESS
ELIZABETH, NJ

During the Great Depression, William A. Kortenhaus was making $1 an hour working as a driver and salesman for Brown's Express of Newark, NJ. When the Depression claimed his job, he had $150 in the bank and his final pay check for $48. The next day, he bought a six year old 1 and a half ton REO, paid $42 for a license and registration fees, put $5 worth of gas and oil in the old truck and had $1 left on which to live. For a total of $197, Kortenhaus was in the trucking business.

His first day in business brought in $28.75 for a run from Newark to Manhatten and return. From his previous job, he knew the suppliers in New York and the auto parts jobbers in New Jersey and soon had 50 customers. When a friend observed that Kortenhaus signed everything "Bill K," he suggested that he call his company "Bill K - Bilkays Express." The year was 1932, and Bilkays became known as the auto parts delivery specialists. With the help of an $800 loan, the fleet was first increased to three and then to ten trucks. Shortly thereafter, Bilkays had its first terminal and it soon housed 20 units.

Still a common carrier during World War II, Bilkays made trips to Curtis-Wright in Caldwell, NJ and to Bendix Aviation and Wright Aeronautics, both in Patterson, NJ. It also hauled from Breeze Metal Hose, which made all of the flexible connections for airplane engines.

In 1945, Bilkays purchased Rollo Trucking's dry freight division from the Nappi family. The next year, the name was changed to Jersey Coast Freight Lines. That same year, the Bobby Corp. (truck leasing) division was formed at Bilkays.

After the war, the company continued to grow and prosper. By 1969, Bilkays operated 140 tractors, 260 trailers, and 104 P & D units operating out of terminals in Newark and Neptune, NJ and Farmingdale, Long Island and New York City, NY. Revenues for the year went over $6 million.

Always an innovator, Bilkays was the first company to use "short doubles" on the New Jersey Turnpike and one of the first to use computerized modules for billing and other time-consuming functions. The company also worked its way into supplying warehousing, distribution services, and truck leasing in addition to its freight operations.

For almost 50 years, the bulk of the company's power units has been supplied by IH with a few Macks thrown in for variety. Equipment has always been meticulously maintained and the Bilkays - Jersey Coast

18

safety record has consistently been an enviable one. (The company has never had a fatal accident to mar its record and no truck belonging to Bilkays has ever been declared "out of service" by a road inspector of the I.C.C.) When the gasoline crunch of 1979 hit, the company began using air shields to reduce wind resistance and steel belted radial tires to reduce fuel consumption.

In 1981, Bilkays formed its dedicated fleet division to service the 3M company. Up until deregulation, the company had enjoyed a 10% return on gross revenues. But after deregulation, profits fell to about 2%. In 1986, the company showed a $250,000 profit on revenues in excess of $22 million.

Incorporated trucking companies and owner operators numbering 9,357 had filed bankruptcy since deregulation in 1980, and Bill Kortenhaus was determined not to be one of them. Changes and hard decisions had to be made, and Kortenhaus was up to the challenge. Jersey Coast Freight Lines, Inc. was merged into Bilkays, one terminal was sold, and the others were leased to Consolidated Freight Lines, Yellow Freight Systems, Carolina Freight Carriers, ABF Freight Systems, and the New Jersey Transit Bus Company. The LTL operation was scaled down to provide personalized service to 35 warehousing customers and 60 distribution accounts were serviced by the warehouse assembly group of

Bilkays.

Today, in addition to being landlord on several freight terminals, Bilkays operates 35 tractors, 50 trailers, and 5 P & D units out of its Elizabeth, NJ terminal. The company offers distribution warehousing and overnight delivery to the greater New York, New Jersey, and Connecticut metro areas, plus extended overnight and second day delivery to all of New England and the Middle Atlantic region.

BILKAYS EXPRESS HISTORY
AND CORPORATE INFORMATION

Bilkays is started on May 31	1932
servicing North Jersey and New York	
Service is extended to South Jersey	1945
Rollo Trucking dry freight division purchased	1945
Rollo Trucking renamed to Jersey Coast Freight Lines	1946
Bobby Corporation formed (Truck Leasing)	1946
Bilkays purchase of Bronx Despatch, adding Long Island	1962
Bilkays purchase of Bronx & Westchester Express, adding New York / Hudson Valley	1974
Jersey Coast purchase of part of Eastern Freightways, adding eastern Pennsylvania	1976
Bilkays purchase of Benton Hartford's Express, adding all of Connecticut	1976
Bilkays Properties formed	1975
Distribution warehouse and service corp. formed	1978
Bilkays dedicated fleet formed	1981
Jersey Coast merged into Bilkays Express	1988
Warehouse assembly group formed	1993
Bilkays Wholsale formed, distributor of Proctor & Gamble products	1994

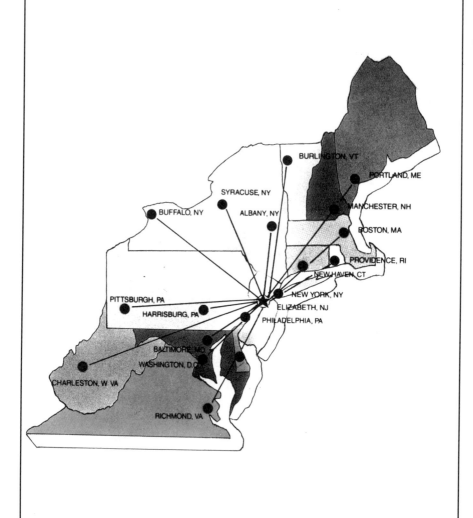

BURLINGTON, VT

PORTLAND, ME

SYRACUSE, NY

MANCHESTER, NH

BUFFALO, NY   ALBANY, NY

BOSTON, MA

PROVIDENCE, RI

NEW HAVEN, CT

NEW YORK, NY

PITTSBURGH, PA   ELIZABETH, NJ

HARRISBURG, PA   PHILADELPHIA, PA

BALTIMORE, MD

WASHINGTON, D.C.

CHARLESTON, W VA

RICHMOND, VA

H. F. CAMPBELL AND SON, INCORPORATED
MILLERSTOWN, PA

In 1925, Harry Franklin "Pop" Campbell built the Keystone Inn on US 22 West. He thought it would make a good stopping point for travelers looking for food, fuel, and lodging. Of the ten available rooms, four were for the Campbell family and six were for tourists. (Room rates were $2 per night, and a hamburger and a cup of soup were 20 cents during the Depression.)

In 1933, Harry and his 20 year old son Ben formed a partnership to purchase a 1931 Ford stake body truck. Harry and Ben alternated driving the truck hauling coal and lumber, while the other one would run the inn. By 1936, they purchased dump trucks and began hauling projects of the WPA (Work Progress Administration) during the depression. The following year, the partnership purchased its first tractor and 20-foot trailer for transporting flour and feed ingredients in an area within 100 miles of Perry County.

During the mid 1940's, the Campbells were granted authority to transport canned goods and both fresh and frozen fruits and vegetables to PA, MD, NY, VA, DC, NJ and DE. By 1956, the company was transporting frozen fruits and vegetables. Equipment at the time consisted of five tractors, 5 trailers, and two stake body trucks. The company also transported farm tractors and equipment, automotive parts, dressed poultry, animal and poultry feed, fertilizer, grain, and insecticides.

In July 1961, the company was incorporated to include Ben's sons in the business. (Harry had sold his half of the business to his son Ben for a nominal amount in April, 1958.) The company continued to grow during the 1960's and 1970's adding frozen fish and banana transporting to its business. By 1977, the fleet increased to 21 tractors, 19 reefers, 10 leased reefers, two dry vans, and one flat. For a brief period, four generations of Campbells worked for the company. Founding father, "Pop" Campbell passed away in August, 1979. Revenues for that year were $2.7 million.

By the end of the next decade, revenues increased to almost $8 million and the company operated over 200 pieces of equipment. During the company's safety banquet in 1990, awards were presented to 49 drivers and workers totaling 407 years of safety and nearly 27 million miles of operation. There were also 15 drivers in the Million Mile Hall of Fame.

Today, the company operates 47 company tractors (mostly T-600 KW's) and 165 reefer trailers and utilizes an additional 22 owner operators.

H. F. Campbell and Son, Inc. operates on theEast Coast and in New England, NJ, NY, IL, IN, KY, MI, OH, MD, VA, NC, and SC.

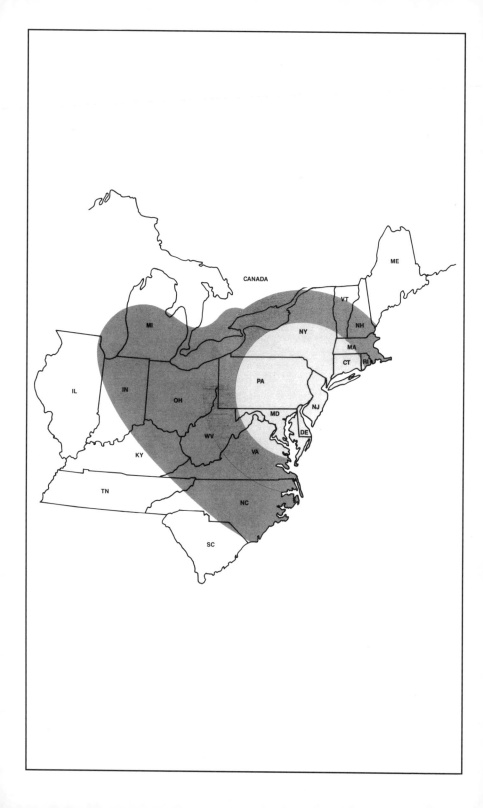

CENTRAL STORAGE & TRANSFER COMPANY HARRISBURG, PA

In 1920, Joseph Garner purchased several small trucking businesses, including the Garis Motor Company. He consolidated his acquisitions and formed Central Storage & Transfer Co. in a small garage and office facility. The Central "fleet" consisted of four International straight trucks, a sizeable fleet for those days.

The "Pyramid of Service" emblem, which had been the trademark of the Garis Company, became the symbol of Central service. The growth of the trucking industry in the 1920's and 1930's was slow; however, acceptance of motor freight service was enthusiastic after World War II. During these years, Central steadily increased the number of vehicles in its fleet and gradually began to expand its service.

Central's original terminal was located at 11th and State streets in Harrisburg. When service was extended to Lancaster and York, terminals were also established in those cities. Central operated a daily overnight service to and from these key points. A second Harrisburg terminal, containing approximately 40,000 square feet of floor space, was erected on six acres adjacent to the Pennyslvania Railroad. This building was completed in July, 1957 and replaced the old 11th street terminal.

In addition to both transporting and warehousing liquor and cigarettes, Central became the connecting carrier for many of the country's leading motor freight companies. Because of the nature of many of Central's loads (cigarettes and alcohol), large markings were painted on the roofs of trailers in an attempt to prevent highjacking.

By 1975, the fleet consisted of 55 single axle IH-2050-A Fleetstar conventional tractors and ten F2010 twin screws, 140 trailers, and 18 IH-1810-A straight jobs. (About 1972, Central switched from gasoline to diesel engines supplied by Caterpillar.) Up until this time, Central's longest one-way run was 125 miles to Scranton, PA. Their average tractor was hooked to three different trailers per day and made an average of 16 stops a day on its peddle run. Shortly thereafter, service was gradually extended to include DE, MD, most of NJ, VA, Washington, DC, and most but not all of PA.

Founder, Joseph Garner passed away in 1978 and his son A. Joseph Garner became president and CEO. John Voystock, who had been brought in by Joe, Sr. pretty much took over the day to day operations of Central until he retired in 1983.

Central was a union carrier and ran into labor trouble in the early part of 1986. There was a strike, which was finally settled, that caused a lot of hard feelings on both sides. In the late 1980's and the first of the 1990's, business began to fall off and Central was losing money. The old union contract was due to expire on March 31, 1991, and union and management said that if the men struck, they would close the doors. The Teamsters struck at midnight on March 31, 1991, and true to its word, Central closed its doors forever on April 1, 1991.

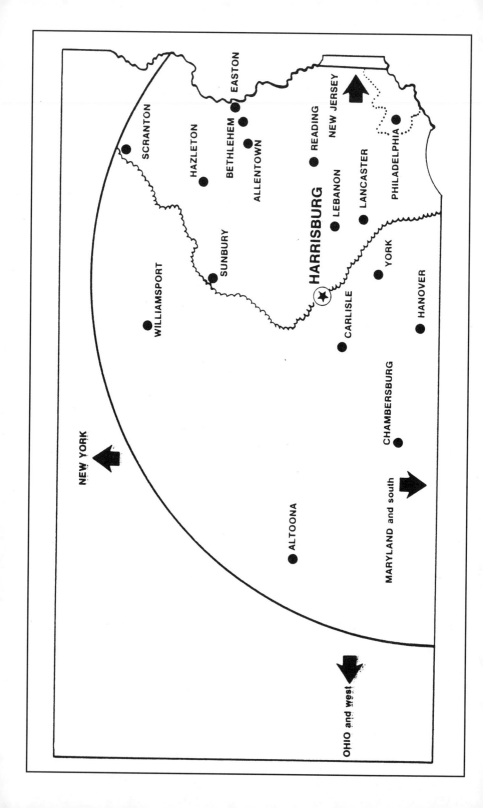

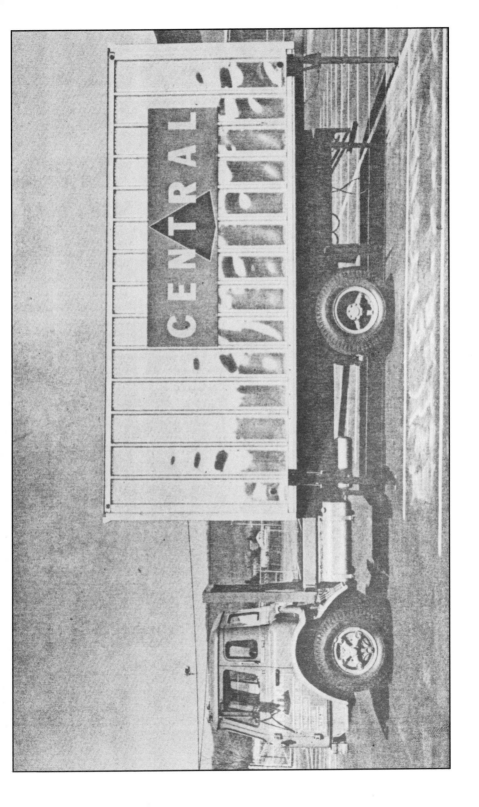

EASTERN FREIGHTWAYS INCORPORATED CARLSTADT, NJ

Nathan Shevell founded Apex Express in 1923 with service in and around the Perth Amboy, NJ area. Subsequent terminals were established in Philadelphia, New York City, and Baltimore. (In 1952, the Philadelphia terminal was moved to Pennsauken, NJ.)

In the 1950's, Nathan's sons Daniel and Myron joined him in the business. At first, they did whatever odd jobs they could find and Apex proved to be the learning ground for the Shevell brothers' future endeavors. The Apex fleet was comprised of mostly Brockway road power with a few Diamond T's thrown in. At its peak, Apex operated close to 100 tractors and almost 200 trailers in its five state operation. (NY, NJ, PA, DE, and MD)

The company grossed almost $14 million in 1962, but when Shevell was unable to come to an agreement with the union the following year, Nathan Shevell elected to retire, shut down the operation, and liquidate assets. After 40 years in trucking, Nathan Shevell may have had his fill, but sons Daniel and Myron "Mike" had just begun their careers.

On July 1, 1963, the Shevell brothers assumed management control of Eastern Freightways. Eastern had been organized in February 1935 as the State Parcel Corp. (The name was later changed to State Freight Lines, Inc.). State Parcel began with one truck operating between the New York City area and the upstate territory between Albany and Utica.

In 1940, Genesee Freight Lines was acquired, expanding operating territory into the western part of New York State. In 1952, the ICC authorized the merger of State Freight Lines, Genesee Freight Lines, and Eastern Freightways. Two years later, Cole Trucking Service was also merged into the company and the resulting firm was Eastern Freightways. Other early Eastern acquisitions included Victor Lynn Lines, Inc., Royal Motor Lines, and Delmarva Terminals, Inc.

The impact of the Shevell brothers was immediate and dramatic at Eastern after they assumed management. Gross revenues exceeded $13.5 million and red ink was replaced with black ink within six months. Eastern's operating territory stretched from Toronto, CN throught NY, CT and portions of MA, eastern PA, and NJ to DE, MD, Washington, DC and VA. Strategically situated throughout the territory were 22 terminals. Other Eastern acquistions included E. J. Scannell, Inc., Niagara Motor Freight Corp. of NY,

Shein's Express of Trenton, NJ in 1965, The National Transportation Co. of Bridgeport, CT in 1967, New York & Worcester Express, Inc. of Worcester, MA in 1970 and Central States Transportation Co. of New York, NY in 1974.

Like Apex Express, the Eastern fleet was made up of a lot of Brockway power, but with all its acquisitions, you could also see lots of Fords, IH's, and Macks wearing the distinctive Eastern colors. By 1972, Eastern operated 700 tractors, 1500 trailers and 205 straight trucks out of 29 terminals in CT, DE, DC, MD, MA, NJ, NY, PA, RI, VT, VA, and Toronto, CN.

The Eastern slogan "On the Ball Service" came about because of the Shevell brothers' interest in sports, not only as fans, but as active participants in various kinds of sports competition. Both listed football and baseball among their favorite sports. Daniel also had an interest in basketball and Mike enjoyed boating. The company also employed several former noted athletic stars in various responsible capacities.

In addition to its freight operation, Eastern also established its carrier rental division, which leased several hundred tractor trailer units and over 1000 automobiles. In 1974, Eastern took on its most ambitious expansion with the acquisition of Associated Transport of New York, NY. Associated was one of the largest trucking companies in America operating over 6,000 units out of 86 terminals. (For more information on Associated, refer to Book I, The Vanishing Trucking Pioneers.) The combined operation of Associated and Eastern Freightways became known as Associated "On the Ball" Transport, Inc. The service area included the states of CT, DE, GA, IL, IN, KY, ME, MD, MA, MI, MO, NH, NJ, NY, NC, OH, PA, RI, SC, TN, VA, WV, and WI, as well as DC and Toronto, CN.

The trucking giant lasted less than two more years when, unable to cover its debts, the company filed for bankruptcy and shut its doors in April, 1976.

NOTE: Eastern Freightways, in its original colors, started a truck load operation out of South Plainfield, NJ in the summer of 1994.

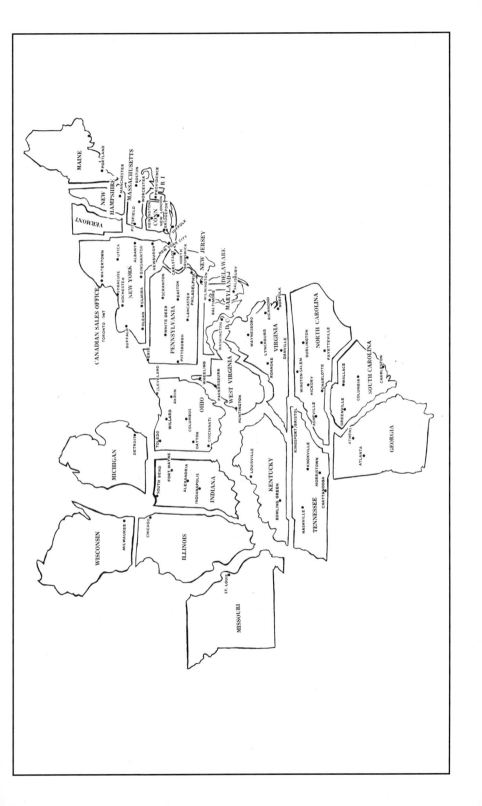

SHIP
BY
APEX
FAST FREIGHT SERVICE
D.P.S.
3165
FRUEHAUF
T-57
APEX

FRIEDMAN'S EXPRESS
WILKES-BARRE, PA

In 1902, Max Frank started his cartage business with horses and wagons on Canal Street in Manhattan, NY. Through hard work, Frank established a reputation for good service and his fledging company began to grow. Joining Frank in his business were his sons Harry, Joseph, and Leonard who all had faith in the future of the emerging trucking industry.

Simon Friedman, a Russian emigrant, founded his transportation company in 1910 using a horse and wagon to pick up freight at the railroad station and deliver it to the local stores. In a happy joint venture in 1931, the Frank family enterprise joined in a partnership with the operation of the Friedman family of Wilkesboro, Simon Friedman and Sons, to launch a successful interstate operation.

Ownership of the company was passed down through four generations of Friedmans and Franks making Friedman's Express one of the oldest continuously operated, family-owned trucking companies in the United States.

Service was extended to include NJ, NY, and PA and interstate service was set up to AZ, CA, CT, DE, DC, HI, MD, MA, NJ, NY, OH, OR, PA, RI, VA, WV, and Puerto Rico. Terminals were located in Allentown, Philadelphia, Scanton, and WIlkes-Barre, PA; Los Angeles, CA, Newark, NJ; Maspeth, Long Island, and New York City, NY; Baltimore, MD; and Cheshire, CT.

At its peak, Friedman's operated nearly 750 tractors and trailers. The early Autocars used by Friedman's gave way to Ford and then Freightliner conventionals. After 60 years of mostly profitable operation, the company suffered losses of $1.2 million for each of the years 1991 and 1992. When Friedman's was asked to pay an additional $370,000 in premiums for its worker's compensation insurance, it was the straw that broke the camel's back. The company file Chapter XI bankruptcy on April 4, 1993, citing debts of $8 to $10 million and assets of approximately $8 million.

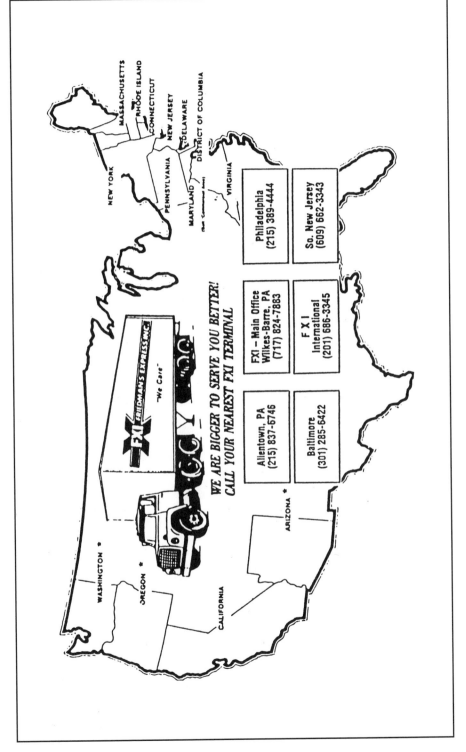

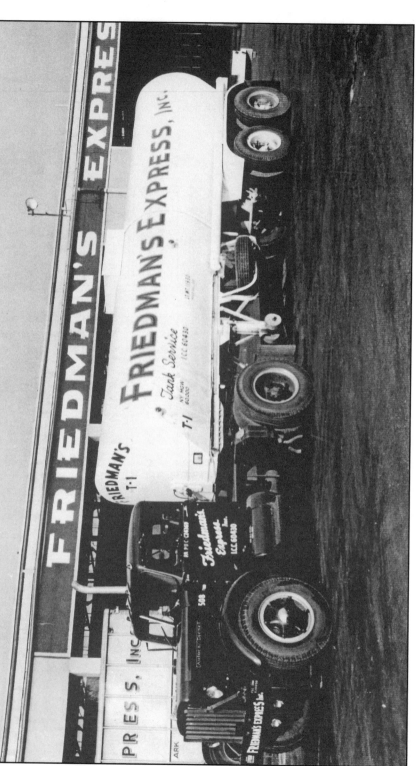

HARRIS EXPRESS, INCORPORATED CHARLOTTE, NC

L. Worth Harris founded Harris Express in the mid 1920's. He built his company on a northeasternly route from Greenville, SC to New York, NY. Terminals were established in Burlington, Charlotte, Gastonia, and Greensboro, NC; Anderson, Greenville, and Spartanburg, SC; Paterson, NJ; and New York, NY.

Harris Express won the triple safety plaque presented by the Motor Transport Bureau three consecutive years from 1951 to 1954. At that time, no trucking line had ever won more than one award at a time. The award recognized the safety and loss prevention of Harris Express in the fields of vehicle accidents, employee injuries, and cargo loss and damage.

By 1954, Harris was operating 101 tractors, 152 semis. and 32 P and D units. Throughout its history, Harris relied on first Autocar, then Mack and White to supply its cab-over and conventional single-axle road tractors. Company equipment was painted dark green (including many trailers) with red wheels and some frames. The impressive road fleet, safety record and routes of Harris Express were particularly impressive to Ryder Truck Lines of Jacksonville who purchased them in 1966.

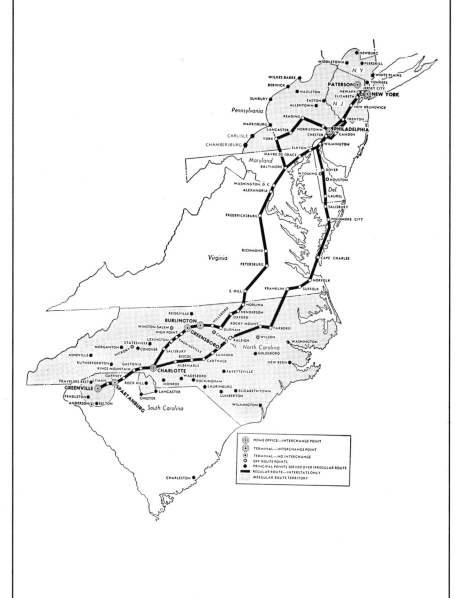

WHITE PLAINS
NEWBURG
PEEKSKILL
MIDDLETOWN
N.Y.
YONKERS
WILKES-BARRE
PATERSON
JERSEY CITY
BERWICK
HAZLETON
NEWARK
NEW YORK
SUNBURY
EASTON
ELIZABETH
ALLENTOWN
N.J.
NEW BRUNSWICK
Pennsylvania
READING
TRENTON
HARRISBURG
NORRISTOWN
LANCASTER
PHILADELPHIA
CARLISLE
YORK
CHESTER
CAMDEN
CHAMBERSBURG
ELKTON
WILMINGTON
HAVRE DE GRACE
DOVER
Maryland
HOUSTON
BALTIMORE
WYOMING
Del.
WASHINGTON, D.C.
LAUREL
ALEXANDRIA
SALISBURY
POCOMOKE CITY
FREDERICKSBURG
CAPE CHARLES
Virginia
RICHMOND
PETERSBURG
NORFOLK
S. HILL
FRANKLIN
SUFFOLK
NORLINA
REIDSVILLE
HILLSBORO
HENDERSON
BURLINGTON
OXFORD
WINSTON-SALEM
ROCKY MOUNT
TARBORO
HIGH POINT
GREENSBORO
CHAPEL HILL
DURHAM
WILSON
LEXINGTON
THOMASVILLE
RALEIGH
WASHINGTON
STATESVILLE
MORGANTON
HICKORY
CONOVER
SALISBURY
North Carolina
ASHEVILLE
BISCOE
SANFORD
GOLDSBORO
RUTHERFORDTON
GASTONIA
ALBEMARLE
CARTHAGE
NEW BERN
KINGS MOUNTAIN
CHARLOTTE
FAYETTEVILLE
GAFFNEY
WADESBORO
TRAVELERS REST
LYMAN
ROCK HILL
MONROE
ROCKINGHAM
GREENVILLE
SPARTANBURG
LAURINBURG
PENDLETON
CHESTER
LANCASTER
ELIZABETHTOWN
ANDERSON
BELTON
South Carolina
LUMBERTON
WILMINGTON

CHARLESTON

HOME OFFICE—INTERCHANGE POINT
TERMINAL—INTERCHANGE POINT
TERMINAL—NO INTERCHANGE
OFF ROUTE POINTS
PRINCIPAL POINTS SERVED OVER IRREGULAR ROUTE
REGULAR ROUTE—INTERSTATE ONLY
IRREGULAR ROUTE TERRITORY

HORN'S MOTOR EXPRESS, INC. CHAMBERSBURG, PA

Horn's Motor Express, Inc. operated under a "Regular and Irregular Common Carrier of General Commodities" certificate subject to the regulations of the Interstate Commerce Commission and the Pennsylvania Public Utility Commission. Regular truck service was provided to points in the United States and the Free World through its own routes or its connections with interline truck carriers, freight forwarders, air freight lines, piggy-back rail service and water carriers.

The company had to make major changes in operation because of the Federal Motor Carrier Act of 1980. As a small carrier, Horn's was especially affected by these changes. In March 1981, Horn's obtained new authority from the Interstate Commerce Commission which permitted direct service between all points in DE, MD, PA, NJ, VA, WV, and DC.

At its peak, Horn's operated 35 tractors, 60 trailers, and one straight truck. Equipment came from Chevrolet, Dodge, Mack, and White and were usually painted gray. After the death of Norman B. Horn on June 20, 1985, the company was managed by a third generation of the Horn family, William N Horn and

Kenneth A. Horn. As was the case with many trucking companies during this time, deregulation was the major cause for Horn's to cease operation in February, 1989.

HORN'S MOTOR EXPRESS, INC.

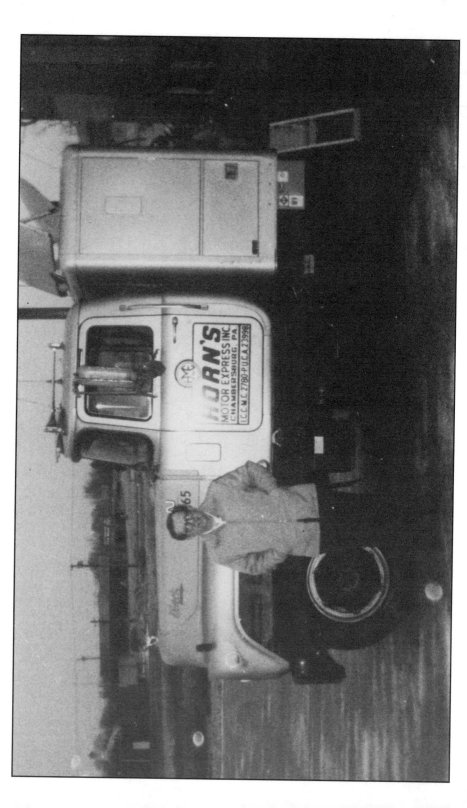

INTER-CITY TRUCK LINES, LTD. MISSISSAUGA, ONTARIO, CN

In 1886,W.K.Colville founded Inter-City Truck Lines Limited as a local horse-drawn cartage business. A large variety of cargoes were hauled, including some loads so large that they required the services of a 20-horse team. When motor trucks began to replace the horse and wagon in 1918, the company began a limited inter-city trucking business between Toronto and Hamilton. This brought about the formation of Intercity Forwarders Ltd, which grew to serve most points in southwestern Ontario.

In 1941, the company was granted authority from the ICC to operate an international service. With this authority, Inter-City began serving most centers in the U.S., interlining with numerous American carriers in Detroit and Buffalo. Inter-provincial rights were purchased in 1952, enabling the company to offer direct service to and from Montreal, and to all points it had previously served in the province of Ontario.

In 1954, it was determined that the company should adopt a more descriptive name. So the entire operation was incorporated under the name Inter-City Truck Lines, Ltd. About that time, Inter-City purchased

C & H Transport Ltd, which served central Ontario and some points in the northern part of the province. By 1960, the company operated 17 teletype-connected terminals and 9 call stations. The Toronto terminal had a full engine re-build shop as well as a continuous-operation tractor and trailer facility. The company also utilized a tractor warm-up shed where electricity heated cold engines. Inter-City was fond of GMC road equipment, utilizing 17000's, DFR 8000's, and D860's in their fleet of 350 tractors. They also ran 374 van trailers, 332 open tops, 22 reefers, 27 heated trailers, and 145 P & D units.

Additional expansion in Canada was accomplished with the acquisitions of Fleet Express Lines, Ltd. and Trans-Canada Highway Express, Ltd. (both purchases taking place in 1973). Trans-Canada was a truck load carrier who in later years operated in the U.S. Ultimately, Inter-City grew to operate nearly 1800 pieces of equipment out of 25 terminals located in the provinces of Ontario, Quebec, Manitoba, Saskatchewan, Alberta, and British Columbia, Canada and U.S. terminals located in Chicago, IL; Detroit, MI; New York City, Rochester, and Syracuse, NY; and Moonachie, NJ.

In the late 1980's, Reimer Express Lines of Winnipeg, Canada purchased the controlling interest in Inter-City Truck Lines, but ran the company independently. Citing a drop in freight going east and west across the country because of increasing north-south trade flows and better service provided by railroad intermodal service, the company closed its doors and liquidated assets in the summer of 1993.

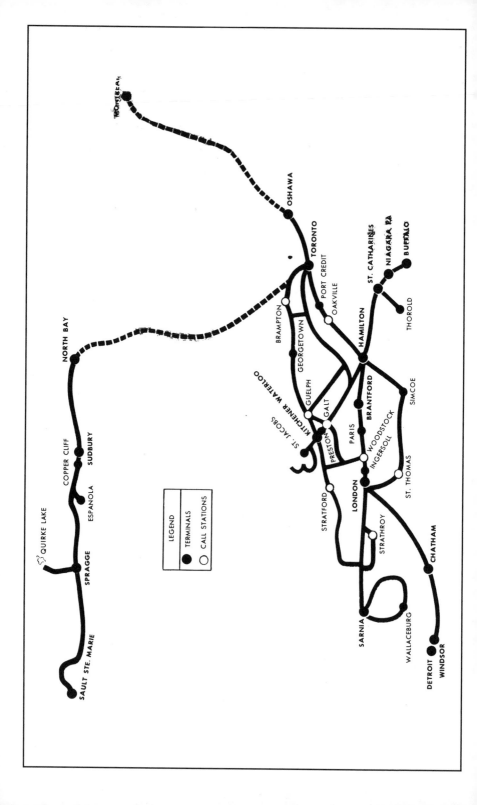

LEGEND

● TERMINALS
○ CALL STATIONS

MONTREAL

OSHAWA

TORONTO

PORT CREDIT

OAKVILLE

BRAMPTON

GEORGETOWN

ST. CATHARINES

NIAGARA FALLS

BUFFALO

THOROLD

HAMILTON

NORTH BAY

GUELPH

GALT

BRANTFORD

SIMCOE

KITCHENER WATERLOO

ST. JACOBS

PRESTON

PARIS

WOODSTOCK

INGERSOLL

ST. THOMAS

COPPER CLIFF

SUDBURY

ESPANOLA

STRATFORD

LONDON

QUIRKE LAKE

SPRAGGE

STRATHROY

CHATHAM

SAULT STE. MARIE

SARNIA

WALLACEBURG

DETROIT

WINDSOR

KINGSWAY TRANSPORTS, LTD. TORONTO, ONT. CN

In 1941, Diamond Truck Division (now Kingsway) was first established with main routes from Quebec City, Three Rivers, and Montreal to Toronto, with spur routes to Ottawa and Sherbrooke. That same year, Beauchamp Express was purchased, giving operating authority between Toronto and Hamilton with all intermediate points.

Over the next four decades, a number of acquisitions took place, continuously extending Kingsway's authority and service. (A complete list of Kingway's acquisitions follows.) With the purchase of Raitar Transport Ltd. of Waterloo in 1952, Kingsway became the first carrier to offer direct service from Windsor to Quebec City. Service was extended into New York City and New Jersey in 1953 with the purchase of Colossal Lines Ltd. Two years later, Maroon Cartage was purchased, providing service to metropolitan Detroit. In 1962, three previously acquired lines, Gossett, Arrow Transit Lines, and Rice and Trimble were merged to form Kingsway Freightlines.

By 1968, the entire corporate organization was restructured with the administration office being located in Rexdale. Operating authority and responsibility was entrusted to four division managers. By this time, Kingsway was already operating 322 tractors, 510 trailers, and 187 trucks out of its 37 terminals. With the acquisition of Nu-Way Express Ltd. of Yorktown, Saskatchewan in 1972, Kingsway had developed operations in each of the provinces from Quebec to British Columbia.

In 1976, Kingsway established Kourier which was a small package carrier with service between Ontario and Quebec. (The company had also established Servall Transports, Ltd. to serve the truckload market in Ontario in 1972.) Three years later, both Servall and Kourier services were extended into western Canada.

By 1981, Kingsway Transports had become one of the largest regulated common carriers in Canada, specializing in LTL freight. Kingsway hauled freight in 1,900 units from Quebec City and New York to Vancouver. In 1986, Consolidated Fastfrate, better known as a freight forwarding company, purchased the shares and assets of Kingsway from Canadian Steamship Lines. This purchase enabled Fastfrate to become a truly North American transportation organization providing various modes of transport to the shipping and receiving public.

Just two years later, the Kingsway group of com-

companies was purchased by the Federated Industries Transport Group which also owned Motorways Canada. Combined, the Kingsway/Motorways group operated more than 100 terminals in central, eastern, and western Canada and in the northeastern seaboard of the U.S.

The two lines were merged at all locations where there was duplication. Kingsway serviced all areas east of Thunder Bay and Motorways services all areas west of and including Thunder Bay. In May 1992, the operating rights of Kingsway Transports Ltd. and Kingsway Transports Inc. were purchased by the Cabano Group of Canada.

KINGSWAY TRANSPORTS LTD.
ACQUISITIONS

Beauchamp Express of Toronto, ONT	1941
Diamond Truck Division of Toronto, ONT	1941
St. Michel Express of Valleyfield, QUE	1943
Pelland Transport of Sorel, QUE	1951
Raitar Transport, Ltd of Waterloo, ONT	1952
Colossal Lines Limited of Montreal, QUE	1953
Maroon Cartage of Detroit, MI, USA	1955
Arrow Transit Line of Toronto, ONT	1957
Gossett and Sons Transport, Ltd of Calgary, ALB	1957
Kuhn Cartage of Buffalo, NY, USA	1957
Drummond Transit Lines, Ltd of Montreal, QUE	1960
Dalewood Transports, Ltd of Hamilton, ONT	1961
Rice and Trimble of Vancouver, BC	1961
Second Transport Ltd of Hamilton, ONT	1961
T.W. Sayle of Hamilton, ONT	1961
Kingsway Freightlines, Ltd of Calgary, ALB	1962
Gaucher Transport Inc of Sherbrooke, QUE	1965
John Kron and Son Ltd ofKenora, ONT	1965
Northern Transports Ltd orf Toronto, ONT	1968
Laurentide Transports Ltd of St. Jerone, QUE	1970
Nu-Way Express Ltd of Yorkton, SAK	1972
Cayer Transport of St. Raymond, QUE	1974
Queensway Transports Inc of Toronto, ONT	1979
Star Transfer Ltd of Timmins, ONT	1984
Yukon Freight Lines Ltd of Whitehorse, NWT	1990

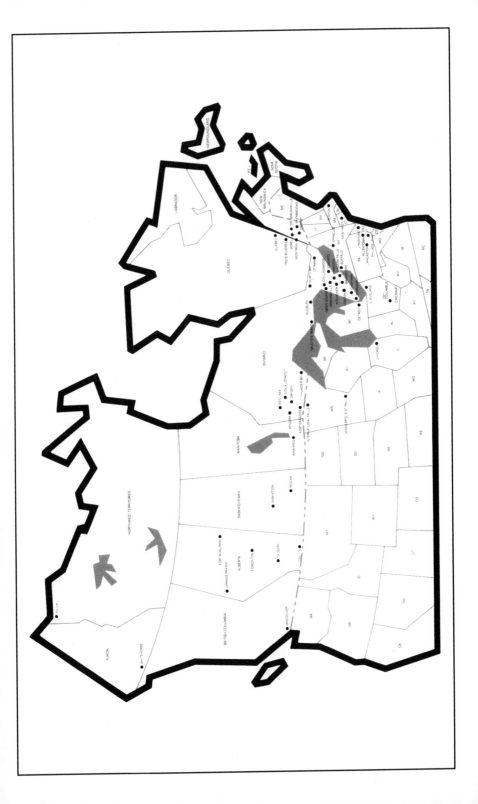

LOMBARD BROTHERS WATERBURY, CT

It all started in 1919 with brothers Nicholas and Joseph Lombard, each with a horse and wagon, competing for delivery assignments at the local railroad station in Waterbury, CT. Within a few years, the brothers joined forces, purchased a pair of used trucks, formed Lombard Brothers, and got into the general freight business.

During the "Great Depression" the company's ability to deliver small shipments to many stores quickly and dependably allowed the Lombard brothers to expand their service and show a profit. Until 1932, all shipments were picked up and delivered within the state of Connecticut. However, seeing the need for a wider delivery area, Joseph Lombard inaugerated "over the road" service by delivering a load to Philadelphia, PA. In 1935, Lombard Brothers was granted ICC certificate MC 42289. (The company was formally incorporated as Lombard Brothers, Inc. on April 4, 1938.)

Lombard's first acquisition took place in 1943 with the purchase of the rights of C. A. Roberts Transportation Co. of Winstead, CT, extending service northeast to the Worcester and Boston metropolitan areas

Five additional operating rights were purchased between 1960 and 1964 and finally in 1968, the rights of Cochrane Transportation Co. of Richmond, VA were purchased to consolidate and enlarge the corridor between Boston and Washington, DC.

Starting in 1961, ten terminals, two modern maintenance shops, and a new headquarters had been built. By 1972, the fleet of two trucks had grown to 185 tractors, 333 trailers, 25 flats, and 115 P & D units. Lombard units were hauling a half million tons of merchandise some 11 million miles and revenues had reached $16.2 million.

During its long history, the bulk of Lombard road power came from four manufacturers: Ford, IH, Mack, and White. The last major purchase of tractors in 1979 was for IH 2275's equipped with the novel thru-lighting concept brightly displaying the Lombard name and wind deflectors. (Lombard had been using wind deflectors since 1969 - long before the fuel crunch.)

In 1973, the company shed its old general offices and completed its new, modern company headquarters. Its completion ushered in the company's golden anniversary in 1974, and the adoption of the new logo, the "Double L." About this time, daily revenues reached $100,000. Another expansion year, 1978, saw additional rights being purchased in Maine with the opening of a Portland terminal in April, and expanded facilities in Baltimore. During the 1980's, Lombard began an agressive tractor restoration program which included new paint and decals, engine overhaul, complete suspension repair, and drive train check-up and repair.

Like many other regional carriers, Lombard Brothers began to lose money after deregulation and the decision to sell the company to North Penn of Lansdale, PA was made in 1984. North Penn operated eight more years before closing down its entire operation on February 21, 1992.

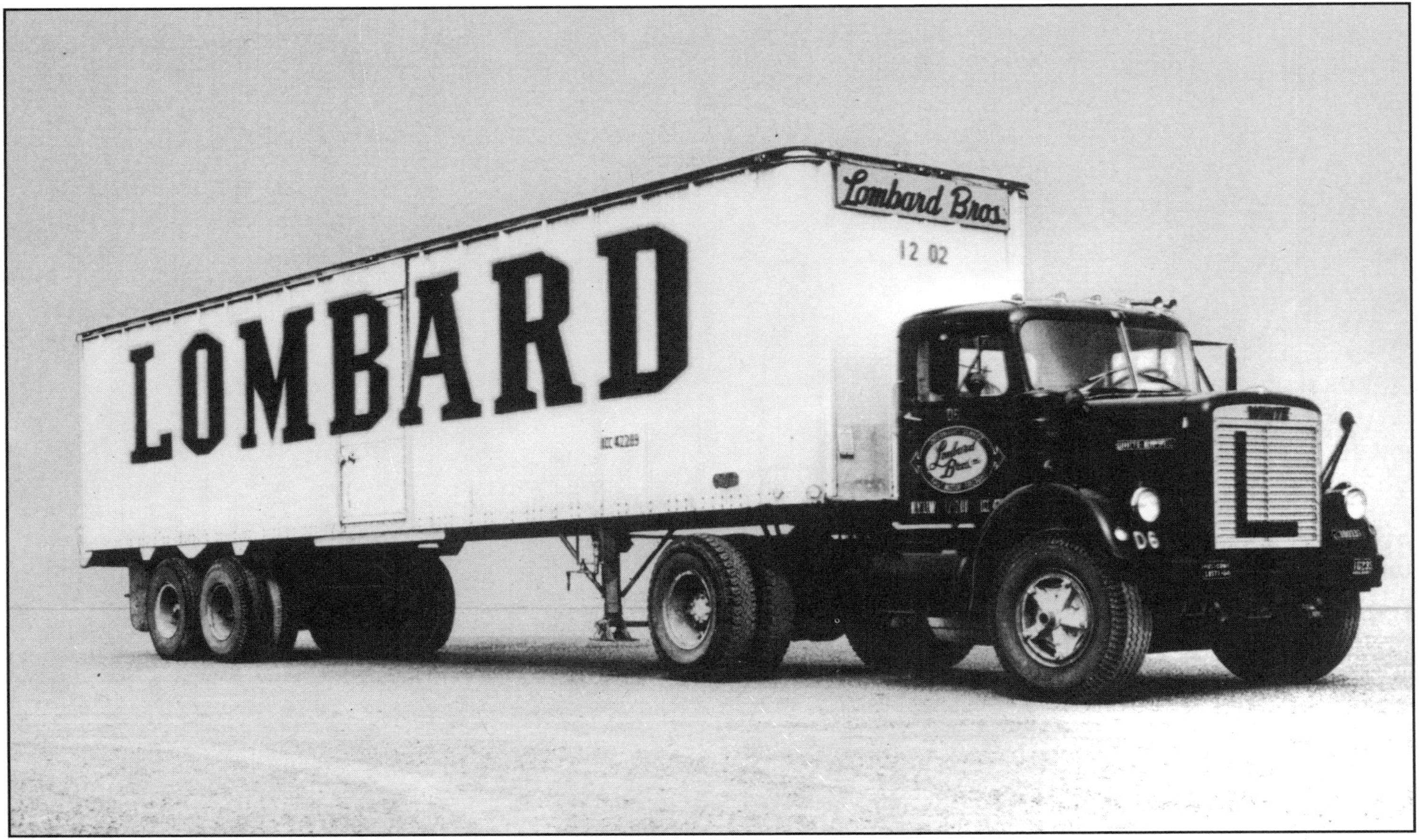
LOMBARD
Lombard Bros.
12 02
D6

MOTOR EXPRESS, INC.
CLEVELAND, OH

In 1930, the O'Neill and Bernet families purchased the rights of what was to become Motor Express, Inc. from Otto Knutson. The ICC MC number granted was #3420. The O'Neills had been in the local cartage business since 1899 and the Bernets got their transportation experience from their involvement with the Erie Railroad. When the Bernet family gained control of U.S. Truck Lines in the mid 1930's, the O"Neill brothers went their own way to form Niagara Motor Express, Anchor Motor Freight, and Signal Delivery Service respectively.

Motor Express grew to offer service in Ohio, western Pennsylvania, and western New York. Terminals were established in Buffalo, Erie, Ashtabula, Pittsburgh, Warren, Akron, Toledo, and Sandusky. Motor Express was a pioneer in handling international shipments from Quebec and Ontario, CN through Buffalo.

In the 1960's, Michigan Express, Inc. laid claim to the use of "MX" as its logo. However, U.S.Truck Line and Motor Express challenged the use of this logo by Michigan Express and won their case in court.

Prior to deregulation, MX interlined freight with Motor Express, Inc. of Indiana (MXI) in Toledo, OH;

the Cleveland, Columbus, and Cincinnati Highway, Inc. (CCC) in Cleveland, OH; and Central Truck Lines in Cleveland.

MX operated primarily White WC22PLT and White 9000 tractors. These were followed by White 9500 and Road Boss tractors. It also ran a few Ford LNT 9000's and some GMC's. City straight trucks were White 3000's and then the White Compact. Trailers were mostly vans with a few open tops used to handle steel accounts in Pittsburgh, Warren, and Youngstown. At its peak, the company operated 115 tractors, 250 trailers, and 40 P & D units. MX had 300 employees and revenues of nearly $15 million in 1979.

The merger of Motor Express, Inc. into The Cleveland, Columbus, and Cincinnati Highway, Inc. was approved by the ICC and took effect on December 15, 1980.

(CCC and MX were both subsidiaries of U.S. Truck Lines and served many common points in northern Ohio and western Pennslyvania.)

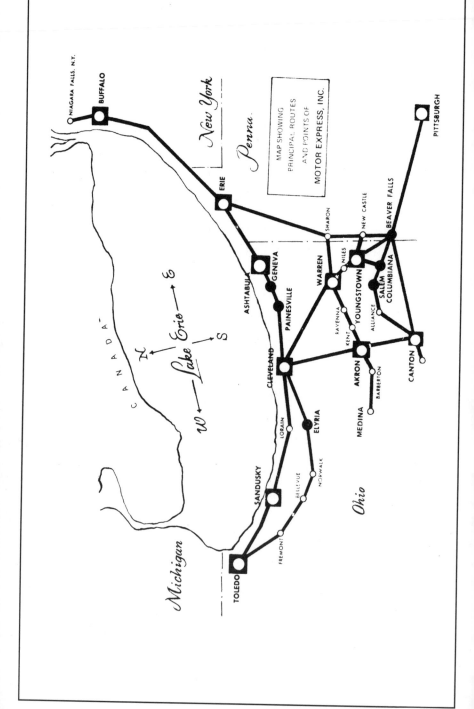

MAP SHOWING
PRINCIPAL ROUTES
AND POINTS OF
MOTOR EXPRESS, INC.

MOTOR FREIGHT EXPRESS SYSTEM
YORK, PA

There are few motor carriers that have compiled a history as long and as progressive as that of the Baltimore Transfer Company - Motor Freight Express System. The Baltimore Transfer Company began operations in Baltimore in 1867 (just two years after the Civil War). The two organizers of the company were named Geoghan and McLaughlin. Originally, the company earned its revenues as a heavy hauling and rigging business, but by the turn of the century, Baltimore Transfer provided pickup and delivery service for a number of large wholesale and jobbing firms in Baltimore.

At its peak, the company operated 50 horse-drawn vehicles. Most of the wagons were drawn by two horses, but 10 and 12 horse teams were utilized in heavy rigging jobs. In 1917, Baltimore Transfer began experimenting with heavy duty, chain-driven trucks. When the new equipment proved to be practical, it gradually replaced the horse teams. (All horse teams were finally retired in 1926.) In 1919, Baltimore Transfer was acquired by the Hoffberger family who would be involved in the operation of the company for the next 60 years. (The Hoffbergers had been operating a coal truck as early as 1913.)

By 1927, the company became involved in the inter-city trucking business with a daily run between Baltimore and Washington, DC. When this operation proved to be profitable, service was then extended north to Wilmington, DE, Philadelphia, Jersey City, and New York and south to Richmond, VA. By 1930, several small carriers were purchased and service was again extended into the central Pennsylvania area. Pennsylvania operations were organized under the name of Motor Freight Express, Inc. with general offices in York, PA. By 1949, BT-MFX System had terminals in Altoona, Baltimore, Hanover, Harrisburg, Jersey City, Johnstown, Lancaster, Philadelphia, Pittsburgh, Reading, Richmond, York, and Washington, DC.

MFX was a very innovative company. With the cooperation of an engineer from the Aluminum Corporation of America, they developed and handbuilt the first practical monocque-type aluminum trailer in 1934. The trailer was then tested by hauling a heavy load of beer between Baltimore and Washington. The company was also a pioneer in communications being one of the first to link up its terminals through a private telephone network. The system's maintenance program was also second to none with well staffed and well equipped shops. For a number of years, these shops also built much of the company's trailer equipment. MFX won several awards for its high maintenance standards, including the ATA's Award for Truck Shop Excellence in 1951, 1953, 1954, 1955, and 1956 as well as the Fleet Owner Award for Maintenance Efficiency in 1957.

Another big expansion period for MFX began in 1965 with the purchase of Cleveland-Pittsburgh Freight Lines, Inc. Next, HCS Transportation of Akron, OH was purchased in 1968. Holland Transportation of Peabody, MA was added in 1970, and Akron-Chicago Transportation of Akron came in 1973. By 1979, BT-MFX had gross revenues of $75.7 million and was ranked the 73rd largest trucking company in America. The company was operating 623 tractors, 1379 trailers, and 55 P & D units out of their 40 terminals. The bulk of the road fleet came from just two manufacturers, International and White.

That same year, a truce was reached with Garrett Freightlines of Pocatello, ID over the title of "the oldest major motor carrier in the nation." The two firms had started operating trucks almost simutaneously in 1913 and agreed to share the title as the two oldest motor carriers in the nation. (Remember that Hoffberger had that coal truck in 1913.)

In 1980, MFX reported net operating losses of

$2.9 million on revenues of $75.2 million. The next year, losses of $3.4 million on revenues of $78.9 million were reported. The following year, MFX had hoped that they would be purchased by Consolidated Freightways who had shown an interest in the ailing carrier. When this purchase did not take place, the company filed Chapter 11 Bankruptcy on October 14, 1982. Less than a month later, the company closed its doors, saying that the combination of the recession and deregulation were the causes of its downfall.

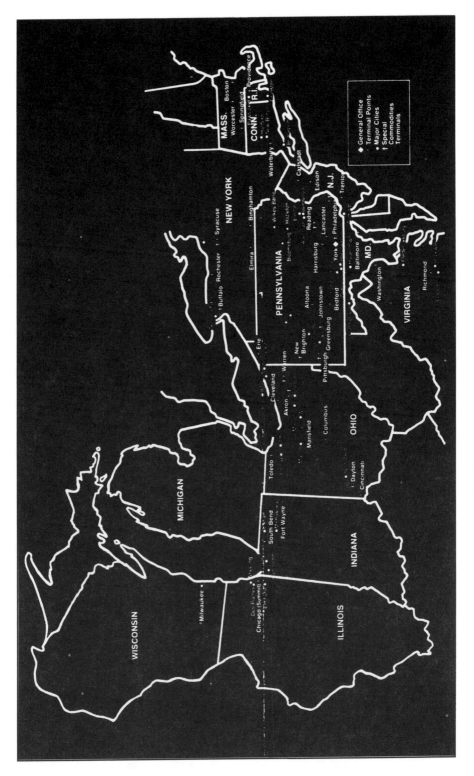

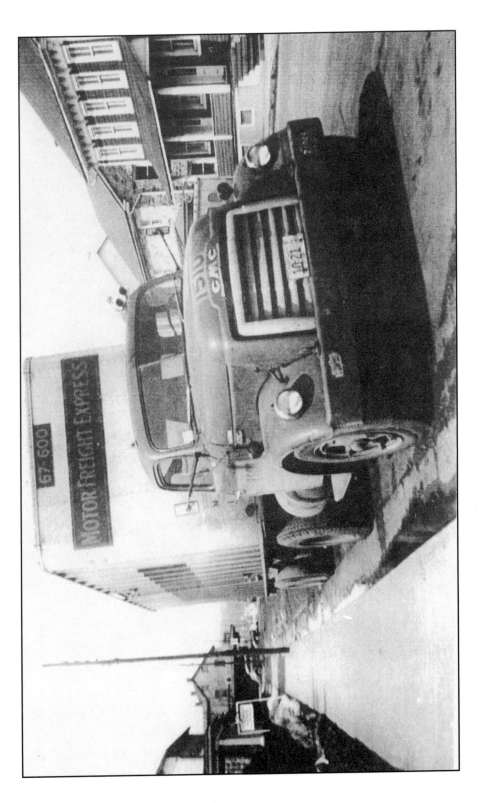

MOTOR
TRANSPORT
MILWAUKEE, WI

George H. Tierman started Motor Transport Co. in 1919 with a single "MASTER" truck. His firm began an inter-city freight service between Milwaukee and Racine (a 28 mile run). In the next 12 years, Motor Transport expanded both its fleet and its territory. During the 1930's, Motor Transport provided feeder service for the Milwaukee Electric Railway and Light Co. (T.M.E.R. & L.) interurban rail line. The success of this co-ordinated rail-truck pick up and delivery effort led to the acquisition of the firm by T.M.E.R. & L. During this period, Motor Transport and T.M.E.R. & L. pioneered the "container" concept - designing and building their own aluminum containers for inter-change-able truck and rail use.

Changing conditions in the industry and abandonment of some interurban lines led to the decision that Motor Transport would confine its operations to over-the-highway service. In 1939, Motor Transport became an independent carrier.

Eventually, service was extended to include 351 shipping points in Wisconsin and Illinois. Terminals were established in Beloit, Janesville, Kenosha,

Madison, Manitowac, Racine, Sheboygan, and Watertown, WI. Motor Transport's main terminal was located on an 11-acre plot adjacent to the Milwaukee Railroad's freight yards in Milwaukee. Company headquarters, freight handling and transfer operations as well as the company's service shops were located there.

At its peak, Motor Transport operated 218 tractors, 406 semi-trailers (vans, tarps, and flats) and 31 P & D units. The company always took pride in its equipment and displayed an impressive fleet of Sterling tractors in the late 1930's. In later years, the road power came primarily from International and White Motor Co.

Motor Transport was a debt-free company, but elected to close its doors effective September 21, 1979 citing deregulation of the industry as its principal reason for shutting down. The company had lost $383,433 on revenues of $11.2 million in the first nine months of 1979.

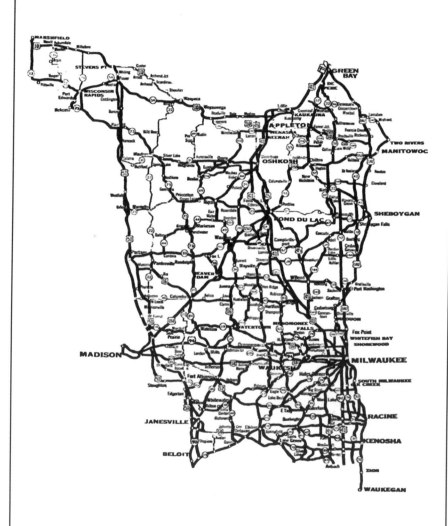

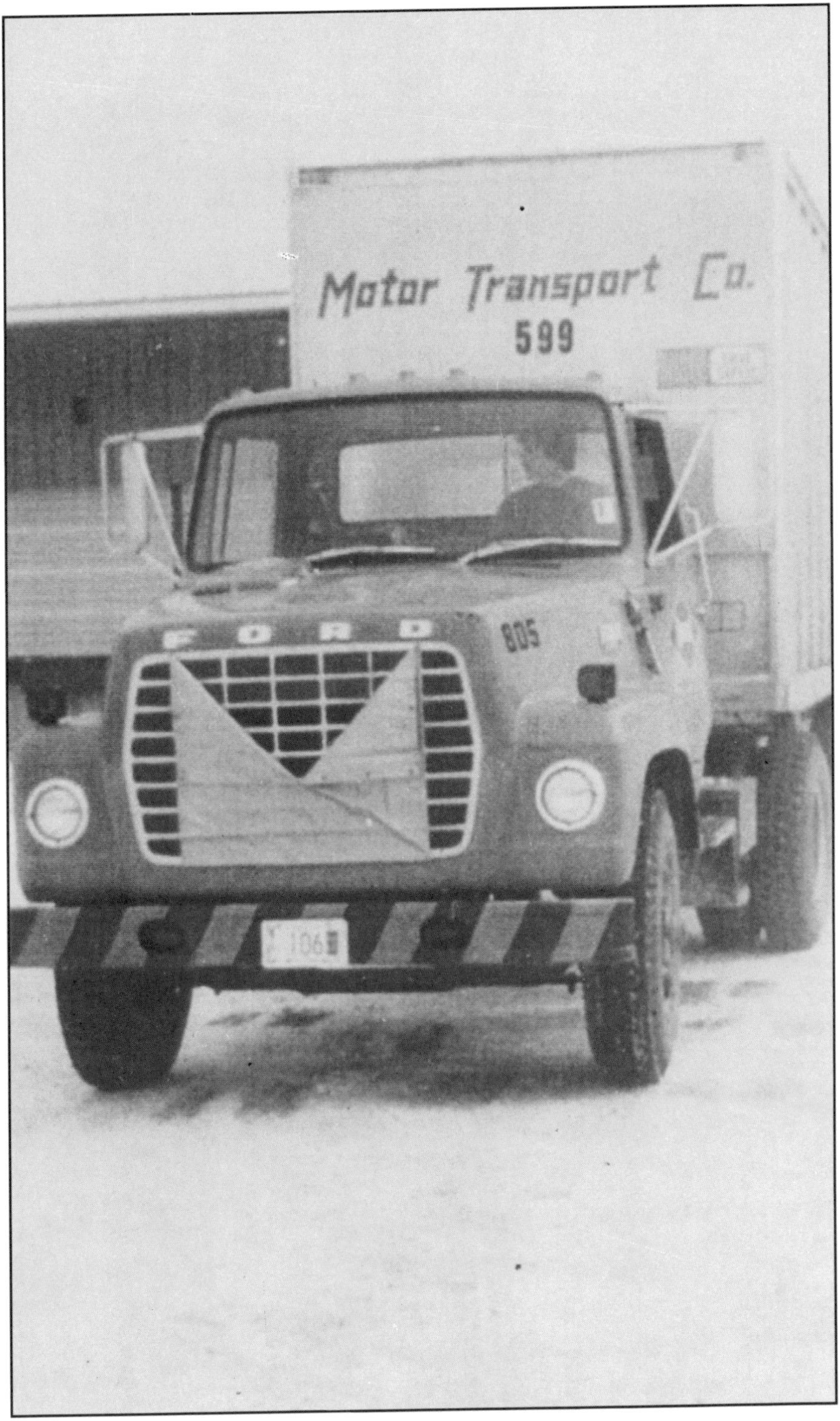

Motor Transport Co.
599
FORD
805

MOTORWAYS, LTD.
TORONTO, ONTAIRO, CN

George and J.S. Hall operated a fuel supply and delivery business within Ottawa and the surrounding area. In 1929, the company was incorporated as Motorways, Ltd. and the Halls began transporting goods between Ottawa and Toronto. Despite some difficult times on and off the road, there was a lot of comraderie in the company. Several company songs and poems praised the service efforts of Motorways and the Halls.

In the 1950's, J. M. (Joe) Atwell of Hamilton came on the scene and became a major force in Canadian trucking by putting several companies together. Atwell had been an associate of the White Motor Company and later owned and managed the Montreal Alouettes of the Canadian Football League from 1966 through 1969. Atwell's first purchase was Hill the Mover, a Hamilton based household goods carrier founded in 1890. Soon after, he purchased Hall's Motorways and Corney Transport of Hamilton. (Stan Corney subsequently worked for Motorways, Ontario, Ltd. in several different positions for the next 54 years.)

Other acquisitions included Motorways, Depot, Ltd. of Toronto; Jackson Transport of Hamilton;

Mason Transport of St. Catherines; Beatty Brothers Transport of Peterborough; Eamer Day of Cornwall (later sold to Direct Systems) and Marcoux Transport of Montreal (the forerunner of Motorways (Quebec) Ltd.). The company was then operated under the name of Hill Motorways. While Mr. Atwell was purchasing freight companies, the British Electric Traction Co. of London, England began investing in the company. By 1956, B.E.T. had a controlling interest and the following year, the company name became Canadian Motorways, Ltd.

In order to bring the east and west together to rival the powerful railways in LTL cartage, Atwell and B.E.T. purchased a number of western Canadian carriers. They also purchased Soo Security, Ltd. about that time. There followed a period during which the company was recognized under various names such as Motorways Van Lines, Hill Security Van Lines, Motorways (Ont) Ltd., Motorways (Que.) Ltd., Motorways (West) Ltd. and finally Canadian Motorways, Ltd. By 1969 the company operated 257 tractors and 320 trailers out of one U.S. terminal in Buffalo, NY and 14 Canadian terminals.

Finally to avoid confusion by the many different names of the company, it was determined that the household goods division would be run under the name "Hill Security Van Lines" while the freight operation was named Motorways. In May 1979, Cougar Freight Systems, a truck load division, became operational. High Tech Express, specializing in transporting time-sensitive high value cargo was launched in 1983. In July 1983, Federal Industries, Ltd. of Winnipeg, through its subsidiary White Pass and Yukon Corp., concluded the deal to purchase Motorways. Soon after Federal sold off Hill Security Van Lines.

Two years later, the company introduced "Motopak," a small package courier service between points in Alberta, Saskatchewan, Manitoba, and northwest Ontario. That same year, in September 1985, Motorways purchased Direct Transportation System Ltd. of Toronto and nearly doubled its size.

In 1989, the purchase of the Kingsway group of companies made Kingsway/Motorways one of the largest transportation companies in Canada. At the time, Motorways operated 4,500 pieces of equipment out of 91 terminals while Kingsway added 2,200 units and 52 terminals to the roster. As was the case with many major failed acquisitions in the United States, the Kingsway purchase may have been more than Motorways could swallow.

The company was losing millions of dollars, so

on July 10, 1992, the Intra-Ontario, Ontario-Quebec, and international portion of Kingsway Transports was sold to the Cabano Group of companies. Continuing to lose money and unable to find a buyer for Motorways, Federal Industries elected to shut down the trucking giant on December 3, 1993.

Three of Federal's other trucking units (Consolidated Fastfrate, an intermodal service, Tri-Line Expressways, a truckload operation, and High Tech Express) continued to operate. All three were profitable and generated annual revenues of about $200 million (Canadian) in 1993.

(A more complete list of Motorways, Security Storage, and Soo Security acquisitions follows on the next two pages.)

MOTORWAYS, LTD. ACQUISITONS

	DATE
HILL MOTORWAYS OF HAMILTON, ONT	
Motorways (Halls) Ottawa of Ottawa, ONT	1950
HILL MOTORWAYS OF OTTAWA, ONT	
Corney Transport, Ltd of Hamilton , ONT	1952
Motorways Depot, Ltd of Toronto, ONT	1953
Jackson Transport, Ltd of Hamilton, ONT	1954
Beatty Brothers Transport of Peterborough, ONT	1955
Eamer Day of Corwall, ONT	1955
Marcoux Transport, Ltd of Montreal, QUE	1955
Mason Transport of St. Catherines, ONT	1955
MOTORWAYS (ONTARIO) OF OTTAWA	
Hill Motorways, Ltd of Ottawa, ONT	1957
Barnhill Transfer of Nova Scotia	1958
Captital Storage of Ottawa, ONT	1958
Moffat and Sons of Nova Scotia	1958
Wilson Transport of Toronto, ONT	1958
CANADIAN MOTORWAYS, LTD OF WINNIPEG, MAN	
Central Transfer of Victoria, BC	1960
Johnson Storage and Cartage of Calgary, SAK	1960
Red Deer Cartage of Red Deer, ALB	1961
Patricia Transportation of Winnipeg, MAN	1962
Prairie Pacific Transport of Edmonton, ALB	1963
Skingle & Sons of Moose Jaw, SAK	1963
Peacock Van and Storage of Regina, SAK	1963
Chapman Transport of Victoria, BC	1965
Mac Arthur and Son, Ltd of Brandon, MAN	1965
Carson Northern of Victoria, BC	1966
Motorways (Ontario) Ltd of Winnipeg, MAN	1983
Soo Security Motorways, Ltd of Winnipeg, MAN	1983
Motorways Direct System, Ltd of Toronto, ONT	1985
CF Kingsway Transports, Ltd of Toronto, ONT	1989

129

MOTORWAYS, LTD. ACQUISITONS (CONT.)

SECURITY STORAGE CO., LTD OF WINNIPEG	DATE
Johnson Terminals, Ltd of Vancouver, BC	1951
Pacific Cartage and Storage of Calgary, SAK	1953
Smeeds Security Storage of Regina, SAK	1954
Big 4 Van Lines of Edmonton, ALB	1955
James Moving and Storage of Calgary, SAK	1955
Soo Freight Lines, Ltd of Winnipeg, MAN	1956

SOO SECURITY MOTORWAYS, LTD OF WINNIPEG

Lewis and Sons Transport of Saskatoon, SAK	1958

SOO SECURITY, LTD OF WINNIPEG

Security Storage Co, Ltd of Winnipeg, MAN	1956
Soo Freight Lines of Winnipeg, MAN	1956

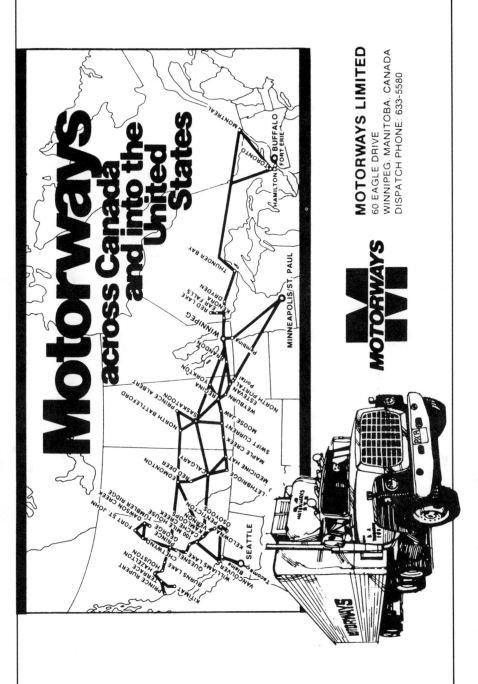

Motorways
across Canada
and into the
United
States

MOTORWAYS LIMITED

60 EAGLE DRIVE
WINNIPEG. MANITOBA. CANADA
DISPATCH PHONE: 633-5580

MOTORWAYS

OAK HARBOR FREIGHT LINES, INCORPORATED AUBURN, WA

Ben Koetje started Oak Harbor Transfer in the year 1916 in Oak Harbor, Washington. The company was purchased by John and Gus Vander Pol in January 1936 for $600 and the following obligations:

A. The balance due on a 1 1/2 ton Reo truck ($800)

B. The balance due on a 1934 four-door Ford sedan ($500)

C. Debt due to Harry Fakkema ($2681).

Oak Harbor mainly hauled full loads of anything within the confines of Whidbey Island, Skagit and Whatcom Counties. About the time Henry Vander Pol joined the firm, in 1937, the company started a daily run to Seattle which got them into the LTL business.

In 1942 Oak Harbor Transfer purchased Oak Harbor Freight Lines and retained that name. Oak Harbor Freight Lines was serving all of Whidbey Island, Seattle, Everett, and Stanwood. In 1947 the company started to serve all of Skagit and Whatcom Counties.

In the late 1960's, John had a stroke and after a long illness passed away. In 1974 Gus Vander Pol sold his portion of the business to Henry. Henry's two sons,

Edward and David, then joined the corporate team. In 1975, Oak Harbor moved its corporate headquarters from Seattle to Tukwila by building a 28-door cross dock terminal, offices, and shop facility. Service was extended to Portland, OR in 1980 and a terminal was immediately opened there as well.

The company took control of Buchanan Auto Freight of Yakima, WA. Terminals were subsequently opened in Pasco, Wenatchee, and Spokane, WA to enable the company to serve the complete eastern side of Washington. In September 1986, partial authority was purchased from Paffile Truck Lines to enable the company to serve the complete western side of Washington. Service was also extended to Longview, Centralia, Chehalis, Aberdeen, Hoquiam, and Shelton. A terminal was then opened in Olympia to better serve the entire area.

By this time, Oak Harbor was operating 35 tractors (a spotless fleet of Fords and IH's), 70 trailers, and 40 straight trucks. In June 1988, authority of McCracken Motor Freight was purchased to expand and serve the I-5 corridor in Oregon. Terminals were opened in Eugene and Medford, OR and the corporate headquarters was moved from Tukwila to Auburn, WA where a new 52-door terminal, offices and shops were built.

Expansion continued in the 1990's. First an IBM A/S 400 system was installed linking all terminals with the home office. Then, two authorities were purchased in Oregon, one to service the southern Oregon coast and the other to serve the I-84 corridor into eastern Oregon. A new 32-door terminal in Portland was completed in June 1991.

The company also instituted the Quality Process to bring better and more competitive services to customers. Also, in December 1991, the company opened a terminal in Reno, NV, their first outside the immediate northwest area. Overnight delivery was offered from Reno to Portland. (This service was not being given on a day-to-day basis by any carrier up to that point.)

New terminals were opened in Boise,ID and La Grande, OR in 1992, giving the company a very comprehensive coverage for Washington, Oregon and Idaho. The following year, terminals were opened in Moses Lake and Bremerton, WA. Yet another terminal was opened in Sacramento, CA in 1994.

In 1996, Oak Harbor Freight Lines is operating 50 line haul tractors, 205 city tractors, 31 P & D trucks, 108 dollies, and 530 trailers out of 19 terminals located in the states of CA, ID, NV, OR, and WA. Also in 1996, the company celebrates its 80th anniversary business and 1997 will mark the celebration of 50 years with the company for Henry Vander Pol.

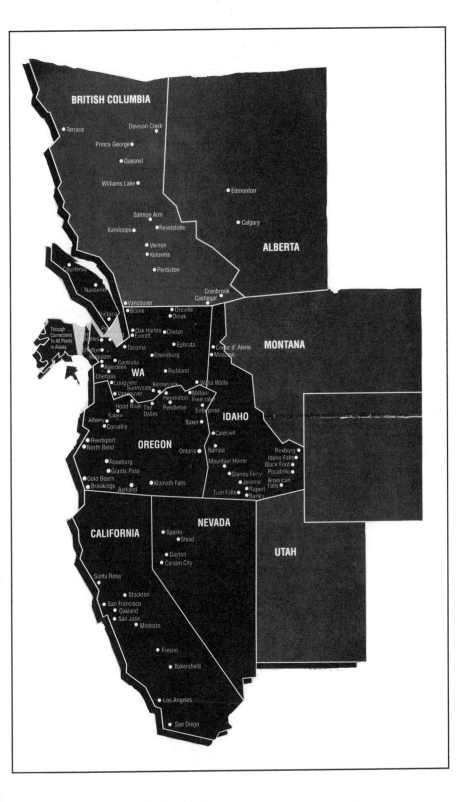

RITEWAY EXPRESS
ELMWOOD PARK, NJ

Riteway trucks first began rolling in 1929. That was the year Harold Kaufman bought out a log hauler named Potter's Express, changed the name, and went into the general freight business hauling for the Whelan chain of drugs. Having survived the depression years, Riteway was granted authority from its home base in Bergen County to the commercial zone of New York City in 1933. Through the war years and into the 1950's, Riteway handled freight out of New York City, largely through a receiving station on Manhattan's Washington Street. The company also became more and more involved with interline shipments connecting with many road carriers. Eventually interline work became the mainstay of the business. In 1957, the company built its first terminal in Westwood, NJ. Prior to that, several makeshift facilities in Westwood and Hillsdale were utilized, including a building up a driveway behind the home of one of Riteway's drivers.

When Harold Kaufman passed away in 1961, his son Charles "Skip" Kaufman - then just 23 - was left to run the company. At that time, Riteway was a small interline carrier with 12 trucks and its entire business rested on interline agreements. However as major carriers opened their own terminals, especially in northern New Jersey, it became clear that the interline business would not always be there. So in 1968, the company jumped in and began competing for short haul business. As it turned out, shippers liked Riteway's high quality pick-up and delivery service. By 1971, the company published a private Riteway tariff.

Meanwhile, at the request of a major customer, Riteway opened its first public warehouse in Carlstadt, NJ. In the mid-1970's, Knorr's Express of Irvington, NJ was purchased. Knorr served central New Jersey and Long Island, NY. Additional rights were acquired to service all of New Jersey and several additional upstate New York counties.

In 1979, the company moved to its new terminal/warehouse in Elmwood Park, NJ. But in four short years, the 30-door facility proved to be too small. So in 1983, the company moved to a 70-door terminal in the Meadowlands, retaining the Elmwood Park building for warehousing. In the early 1980's Riteway's maintenance department performed minor repairs as a courtesy for one of the local companies. Realizing that their own equipment was in above-average shape and that there was a high level of maintenance skills within the company, Riteway began a new revenue source, a separate maintenance-for-hire profit center. Within two years, the company had 22 individual maintenance agreements with local small fleets.

In 1986, the trucking operation moved back into the Elmwood Park facility which is the company's current headquarters. Today Riteway utilizes 280 pieces of equipment and services Maine to Virginia with four terminal locations: Paulsboro, NJ; Wallingford, CT; Wobern, MA; and Elmwood Park, NJ.

Over the years, the Riteway fleet has been made up of Ford, IH, Mack, and White road power. The newest addition however, is made up of F670 matched conventional Freightliners and WG 64T Volvo White straight trucks in the new company white with green and black letters. Riteway and its subsidiaries, Nustar Service, Inc, (a 48-state truck load operation); Surety Warehouse Services, Inc. (public warehouse facility); and Perfect Fit Warehousing (a footwear distribution center) generated revenues of $14 million in 1993 and $16 million in 1994. They are expected to top $20 million for 1996.

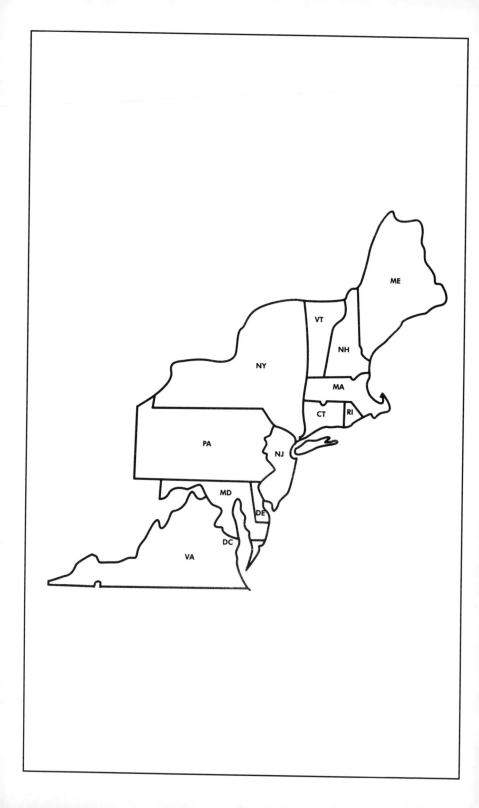

Classic

Photo's

RUZILA'S EXPRESS SERVICE, INC.
GARFIELD, NJ

It all began in 1909 when Paul Ruzila drove his horse and wagon to pick up coal to heat the homes of friends in Passaic, NJ. Local people then began hiring him to transport other products. Ruzila's two sons, Peter and John, saw a future in the business and in 1926, they purchased their first motor vehicle. The business gradually grew and soon call stations were established in Boston, Bridgeport, Baltimore, and Washington, DC.

Ruzila's was instrumental in helping to build the George Washington bridge, linking NJ and NY, by transporting construction materials to the site between 1927 and 1931. Ruzila is proud to say that it was one of the founding fathers of the American Trucking Association and of the New England Motor Rate Bureau.

Because of the shortages during World War II, it was decided to limit operations to New Jersey, metro New York, and New England. In 1945, the company moved from Passaic to Garfield, NJ. In 1948 operations were moved from Boston to Blackstone, MA to be closer to the textile industries in Woonsocket, RI. (Ruzila's still operates from both of these locations.) Ruzila's specializes in LTL service, but also handles TL shipments in NJ, CT, MA, RI, and portions of NH, ME, and PA. In New York, the company serves the five boroughs and Long Island as well as Rockland and Westchester counties.

Ruzila's early Brockways have given way to the current fleet of 10 Mack tractors. The company also utilizes 28 trailers of various makes, ranging from 27 to 48 footers. The company has come a long way since the horse and buggy days, but John's sons still operate under their grandfather's philosophy, "Stay small and treat everyone as family."

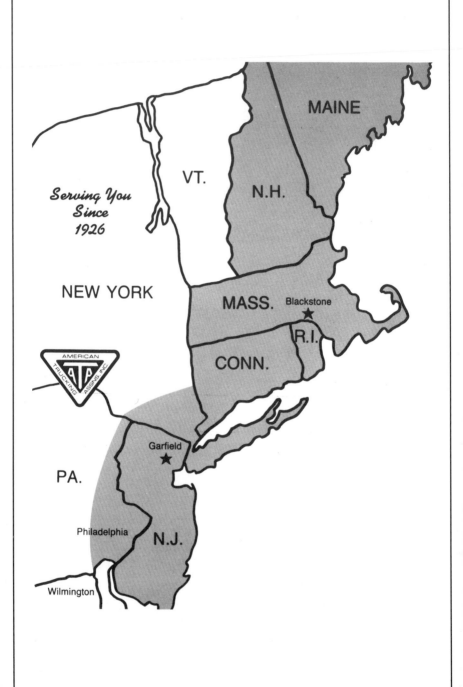

RUZILAS
RUZILA'S EXPRESS SERVICE
167 FOURTH STREET
PASSAIC, N. J.
TEL. PASSAIC 2-8959
T-2
RUZILA'S
EXPRESS SERVICE
Passaic, N. J.
D.P.S. 4121

SCHERER FREIGHT LINES, INC.
OTTAWA, IL

Thomas Scherer started his local horse-drawn dray service in 1863. He dealt in coal, building materials, fuel, oil, ice, a soft water service, and local cartage. By 1900, the Scherer family business had 120 horses in its barns. They bought their first truck in 1907 and their second was added in 1910. Thus began a rapid mechanization of equipment.

From the family business, the third generation of Scherers, Alexander and Walter, founded Scherer Freight Lines of Ottawa, IL in 1931. Early over-the-road operations included hauling equipment to the Chicago World's Fair in 1932 as well as hauling glass marbles to other states. General freight operations were in northern and eastern Illinois.

In two early acquisitions, Scherer first purchased the I.C.C. authority of Chicago-St.Louis Transfer of Springfield, IL and St. Louis, MO and then purchased I.C.C. authority of Lloyd Merkel of Aurora, IL. These transactions extended their authority to northeastern Illinois, Milwaukee, and southern Wisconsin. The result was a sizeable operation which included Aurora, Bloomington, Chicago, Decatur, La Salle, Ottawa,

Peoria, and Rockford, IL as well as St. Louis, MO and Milwaukee, WI. Later, a steel division terminal was also located in Hammond, IN.

In 1958, Scherer took over the operations of Decatur Cartage Company in IL and St. Louis, MO, but did not acquire the I.C.C. authority as it largely duplicated that of Scherer's. (All of the Decatur I.C.C. authority was acquired by Decatur Seaway Motor Express on October 11, 1958 and by Transcon Lines on June 30, 1965.) On November 22, 1967, Associated Transport acquired the authority and operations of Scherer Freight Lines. At the time, Scherer operated 285 tractors, 400 trailers, and 68 P & D units throughout its six state operation in IL, IN, IA, MO , OH, and WI. (For more information on Associated Transport, see Book I of the Vanishing Trucking Pioneers.)

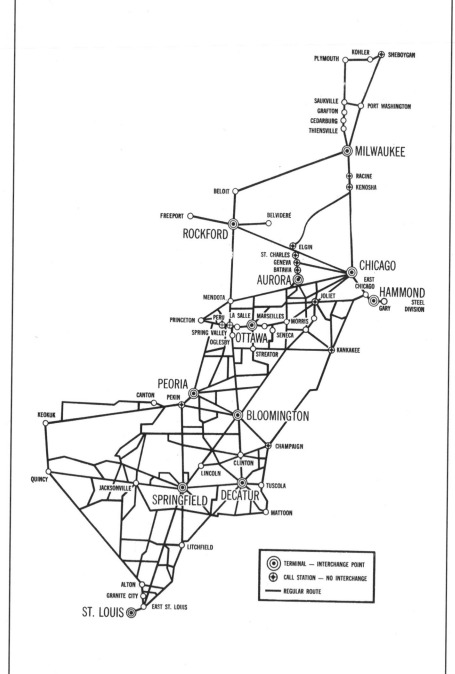

TERMINAL — INTERCHANGE POINT
CALL STATION — NO INTERCHANGE
REGULAR ROUTE

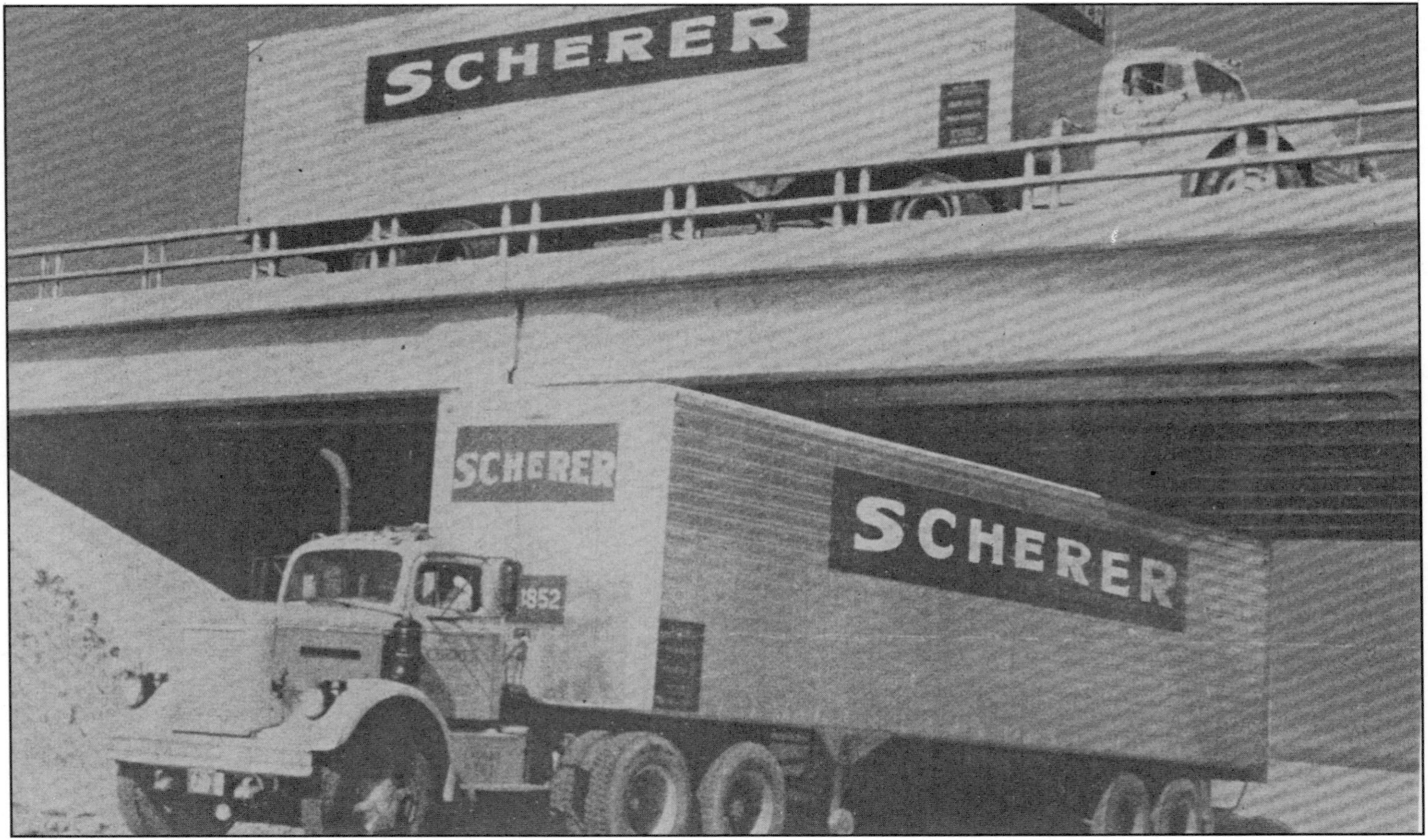

STERLING TRANSIT COMPANY INCORPORATED MONTEBELLO, CA

Sterling Transit Company was established in 1933 by Orin Thorkildsen. Throughout its 56 year history, the company remained strickly a California carrier and enjoyed a steady rather than spectacular growth. By 1962, Sterling was still a modest sized carrier, operating 26 diesel tractors, 68 gas tractors, 59 bobtails, 22 stake trailers, and 136 vans. Original colors were red, black, and white tractors and silver trailers.

Some of the Sterling drivers took so much pride in their company tractors, that they invested their own time and money adding chrome and keeping the company trucks in tip-top condition. Thorkildsen was a collector of classic motor vehicles and had one of the largest and best private collections of historic automobiles and trucks in the U.S.

In 1975, Thorkildsen sold the company to an employee group but remained chairman and president until 1984. Two years later, Jerry Lundbergh purchased the company from the stock ownership group. The following year, the employees took a 13% wage cut to help the ailing carrier, but the company still lost $36,000 on revenues of $16.8 million for the year.

At its peak, Sterling employed 300 men and women and 150 drivers. They operated a total of 700 tractors and trailers, utilizing GMC, IH, KW, Mack, and White road power which was painted in Sterling's new brown. Sterling's eight California terminals were located in Los Angeles, San Leandro, Sacramento, San Jose, Stockton, Fresno, Bakersfield, and San Diego.

When the company continued to lose money, citing heavy competition from non-union carriers, the decision was made to shut down the operation and liquidate on November 6, 1989.

STRICKLAND SYSTEM DALLAS, TX

In 1930, L.R. Strickland founded Strickland Transportation with original authority serving points in Arkansas and Texas. The company remained a relatively small regional carrier until the mid 1950's when major expansion took place through acquisitions.

The first of the purchases was Dumont Cartage Co., Inc. of Aurora, IL in 1956. Next came Kelleher Motor Freight Lines, Inc. of St. Louis , MO in 1957. Kelleher operated from St. Louis to Chicago and then Cleveland to New Jersey and also had authority direct to Cleveland via Indianapolis. Strickland operated the new authority as one truck line, but maintained a separate corporation for years and reported the revenues as Strickland Motor Freight Lines, Inc.Their major shop operation and break bulk was in Little Rock, AR. East Central Motor Freight of New Jersey and Burks Motor Freight Line of Little Rock, AR were both added in 1958 and Michigan Tri-State Motor Express, Inc. of Benton Harbor, MI came in 1959.

Service was being established from the west on a north-east line to Boston with routes through Chicago and New Orleans from the south. By 1965, Strickland operated 35 terminals in 16 states including AR, CT, IL, IN, LA, MA,MI, MO, NJ, NY, OH, OK, PA, TN, TX, and WI. Gross revenues for the year reached $31 million and Strickland was listed as the 35th largest motor carrier in the U.S.

The Strickland fleet grew to 477 tractors, 980 vans, and 105 open top trailers. In the 1940's and early 1950's, road power came primarily from the White Motor Company. In the mid 1950's the company sported 32 matching B61T Mack tractors among the fleet. The 1960's saw a lot of cab-over IH's in service and finally scores of cab-over Freightliner tractors were utilized.

By 1968, L.R. Strickland sold his company to Hill & Elliott Associates of Dallas, TX. The Strickland System would never be the same again. In the 1970's, the company experimented with 12' x 12' modular units with individual sleeping rooms and private baths for road drivers. This innovation, however, could not stem the red ink which began appearing on the books. By the mid 1970's, the system was losing substantial amounts of money, citing the downturn on the economy. Strickland fought for several more years before selling all outstanding company stock to the Wilson Freight System of Cincinnati, OH in 1978 for a reported $4 million.

Wilson's was able to operate just two more years before its own financial problems forced the company into bankruptcy on July 23, 1980.

STRICKLAND SYSTEM ACQUISITIONS

Ozark Motor Lines of Arkansas	1946
Eddy Freight Line	1947
Fraps Truck Line	1947
Gordon Interstate, Inc.	1948
Dumont Cartage Co., Inc. of Auror, IL	1956
Pittsley, L.W. of Iowa	1956
Kelleher Motor Freight Lines, Inc of St. Louis, MO	1957
East Central Motor Freight, Inc of New Jersey	1958
Burks Motor Freight Lines, Inc. of Little Rock, AR	1958
Michigan Tri-State Motor Express, Inc. of Benton Harbor, MI	1959
Eaton Truck Lines, Inc. of Windsor, MO	1965
England Transportation Co., Inc. of Dallas, TX	1965
Tracy Trucking Co. of Ohio	1965

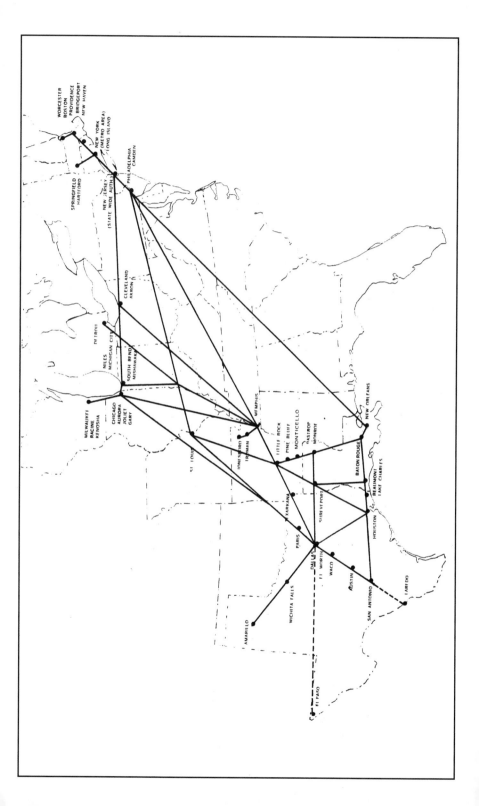

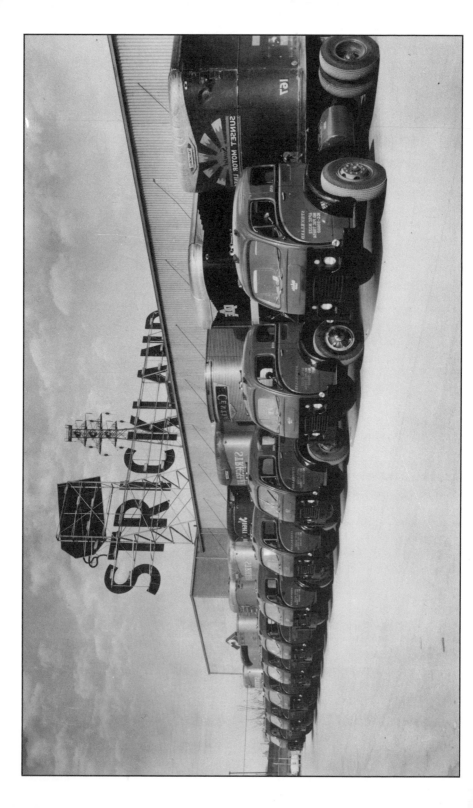

CROCKETT
HOTEL
SHIP
STRICKLAND
TRANSPORTATION
CO. INC.
TEXAS ONIONS
FOR CONGRESS
New Crop... Now Ready!
GRANEX BERMUDAS GRANOS
Fresher ... Milder ... Sweeter ...
1171
1171
732
STRICKLAND

SYSTEM 99
INTERLINE-BLANKENSHIP
MOTOR EXPRESS
OAKLAND, CA

When Montgomery Ward established its Oakland plant in 1923, L.M. Blankenship purchased a truck and contracted to haul merchandise for the firm in and around its base of operations. Two years later, the company had four units roaming the California highways.

Blankenship Motors was incorporated in 1928 with J.M. Blankenship as its first president and Louis A. Dore, Sr. (who would succeed J.M. in 1935) as vice president. Together they built the company to employ 200 men and women operating 187 units throughout the state of California. (Blankenship units went up to 300 miles north of Oakland, 175 miles east and 600 miles south.) Blankenship used big International road power (primarily L-405 and LD-405 Roadliners) in its fleet. Extensive use was made of 22-foot sets of doubles to haul "just about everything except livestock."

Marvin D. Gilardy and E.R. "Red" Preston owned Interlines Express, another California carrier (established in 1928 as G & H Motor Express), with a lot of business, but with a lack of equipment and terminals.

200

When Dore lost the Montgomery Ward account, he wound up with lots of equipment and terminals, but no business. In 1963, Gilardy, Preston, and Dore merged their assets and formed Interlines - Blankenship Motor Express, a perfect marriage. At the time of the merger, the combined fleet numbered nearly 500 units.

Marv Gilardy of Interlines became president and Red Preston, also a partner at Interlines who had driven every one of the company's trucks in his long career, took over the overall operations of the "99" fleet. Lou Dore, who operated Blankenship, had the responsibility for reporting on operating, the company's financial status, and the company's complex insurance program. Ed Maroder, who was recognized as one of the most astute controllers in transportation, organized fiscal and office operations and had complete authority over all budgets. He brought in Meade Bridgeman and Ray Mitchell who were experts in computers and management. With this management team, the company had earned the best operating ratio among the state's LTL common carriers by 1964.

By 1969, the company operated 224 tractors, 454 trailers (391 vans and 63 flats) and 120 P & D units out of its 25 California terminals. About this time, the company purchased Bay Freight Lines of Arcata, CA. The company had officially become "System 99" in

1968. When asked why the "99," Red Preston said "The Chinese say 99 means good luck." Marv Gilardy said, "It means 99 reasons you should ship by our service." Others said it could mean the old Highway 99 from where the company grew. Whatever the explanation, System 99 was on a roll and shippers knew who "99" was.

Interlines remained a California carrier until July 1974 when it purchased Transwestern Express of Oregon (formerly named the Bend-Portland Truck Service). The company had been interlining with Bend-Portland for some time. Also in the mid 1970's, service was expanded into Nevada with the purchase of McCloud Transportation. Revenues for 1977 reached $65 million and System 99 ranked among the top 50 carriers in the U.S. System 99 grew to operate 34 terminals in their 11 state service area which included AZ, CA, ID, NV, NM, OR, TX, UT, and WA.

At its peak, 99 used 264 line tractors, 400 city tractors, 95 bobtails, 1347 van trailers, 5 reefers, 29 flats, and 448 dollies. International Harvester was the primary provider of road power, but lots of Freightliners and Macks were on the roster.

Hurt by re-regulation in 1980 System 99 was never again a profitable carrier. having become over-extended with the banks over the next few years, the company filed bankruptcy and liquidated all assets in 1987.

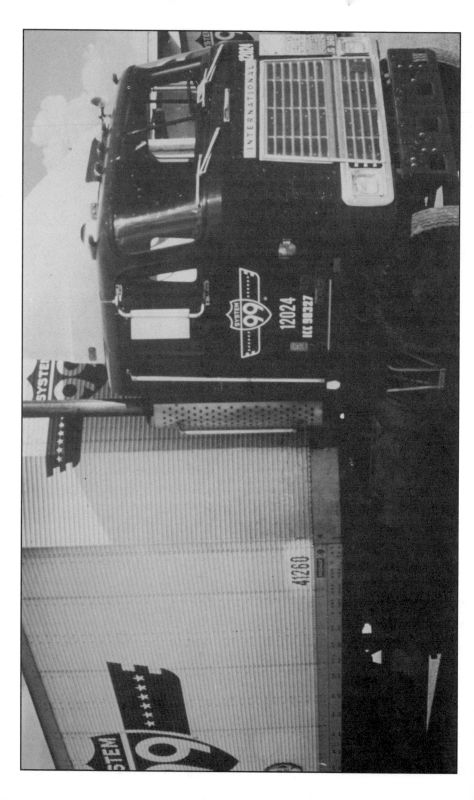

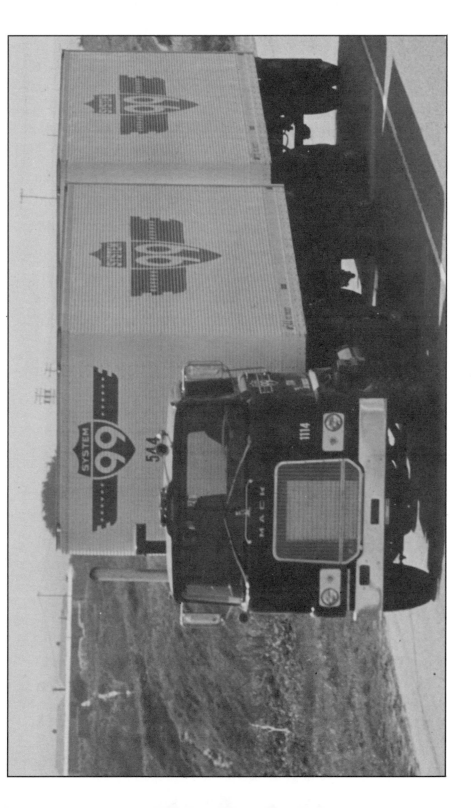

TNT RED STAR EXPRESS, INCORPORATED
NEWARK, NJ

In the 1920's John Bisgrove, then in the seventh grade, "borrowed" his father's gold watch and swapped it, along with a hutch of pet rabbits, for a horse named "Happy." With Happy, who turned out to be blind in one eye, Bisgrove began hauling his neighbor's stove ashes, wood shavings, and groceries around his small, upstate New York hometown of Auburn. In 1932, John married his hometown sweetheart, Irene Nolan. On their wedding day, the young groom presented his new bride with her wedding gift - a bright red 1932 Dodge Brothers truck. Red Star Express was born.

Red Star's first routes served Auburn, Syracuse, and New York City. John's brother, Leonard Bisgrove, drove the first Red Star truck that went to New York. Although Leonard only planned on staying in New York for about a month, he quickly saw opportunities there, settled down, and devoted his career to developing what is today Red Star's major metropolitan market.

During the Depression, Red Star's freight volume grew steadily. The railroad's restricted schedules could only accomodate full carloads, leaving less than carload shipments to the trucking companies.

John Bisgrove's straightforward business philosophy contributed greatly to Red Star's growth. "Freight delivered on time and in good shape" was the motto that served Red Star well. Between 1932 and 1961, Red Star expanded in upstate New York and New Jersey, opening terminals in Rochester, Syracuse, Buffalo, Utica, Jamestown, Albany and North Bergen, NJ. By this time, gross revenues exceeded $10 million. In 1961, Red Star began a series of acquisitions and mergers that extended its operating authority and expanded its coverage to blanket the northeast:

-John Vogel, Inc. 1961, extended authority into Philadelphia, eastern NY and western MA

-Brown's Express, 1964, extended authority to Boston from Albany

-Wallace Transport, 1967, extended authority into Ontario province

-P.S. Dubrey Trucking, 1968, extended authority in New York state from Glen Falls to the Canadian border

-Laurel Transport, 1969, extended authority into Quebec province

-Marcoux Transit, 1975, expanded coverage in Quebec province

-Tidewater inland Express, 1979, extended authority into DE, central PA, and Maryland's eastern shore.

While growing, Red Star also was innovating.

The first "double bottoms," the tandem trailers that are a common sight on interstate highways, were pioneered by Red Star, and today Red Star uses more of them than any other trucking company in the Northeast. Red Star was also one of the first U.S. carriers to enter the Canadian market in 1962. By 1980, the company entered the exclusive club of U.S. carriers exceeding $100 million in gross revenues.

TNT Limited of Sydney, Australia purchased Red Star in June of 1987 and TNT Red Star became part of a worldwide group of transportation companies.

In February 1992, TNT Freightways became a publicly traded company, separate from TNT Limited, which offered complete U.S. coverage with TNT Red Star, TNT Bestway, TNT Holland, TNT Dugan, TNT Reddaway, and TNT United.

1995 was an aggressive expansion year for TNT Red Star starting with the completion of a new 94-door terminal in Cumberland, RI in January. In February, terminals were opened servicing both North and South Carolina. In April, TNT Red Star opened a terminal in Atlanta, GA. Another terminal was opened in Columbia, SC in August.

In addition, $14.3 million of revenue equipment was delivered to the fleet in 1995 (104 road tractors,

100 city tractors, and 200 trailers).

Today, TNT Red Star operates with nearly 1000 tractors and 2200 trailers and employs 2400 men and women. TNT Red Star covers 16 states offering direct service to almost 20,000 points from Portland, ME to Atlanta, GA.

In 1994, revenues reached $180 million with 1995 revenues expected to approach $200 million.

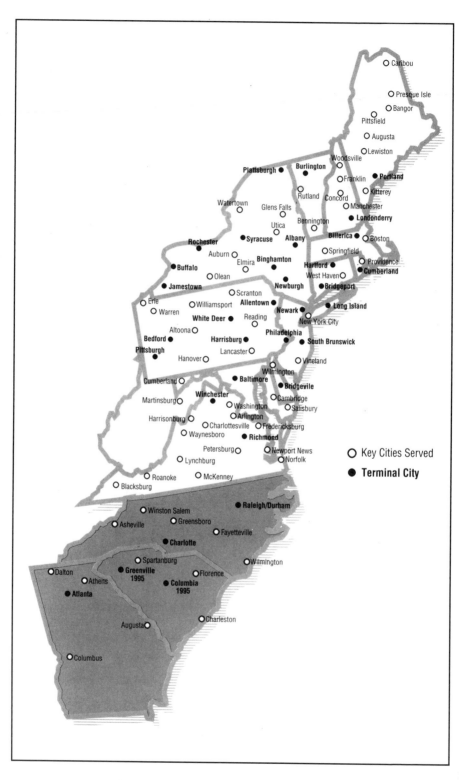

O Caribou

O Presque Isle
O Bangor
Pittsfield
O Augusta
O Lewiston
Woodsville
Plattsburgh ● ● Burlington
● Franklin ● Portland
O Kitterey
Rutland Concord
O Manchester
Watertown Glens Falls Bennington ● Londonderry
Utica
Rochester ● Syracuse ● Albany Billerica ● O Boston
Auburn O ● Springfield
Buffalo ● Elmira Binghamton Hartford ● Providence
Jamestown ● Olean West Haven O ● Cumberland
Newburgh ● Bridgeport
Erie O Scranton
Warren O Williamsport Allentown ● Newark ● ● Long Island
White Deer ● Reading New York City
Altoona O
Bedford ● Harrisburg ● Philadelphia
Pittsburgh ● Lancaster O ● South Brunswick
Hanover O
Vineland O
Cumberland O Wilmington
Baltimore ● ● Bridgevile
Martinsburg O Winchester ● Cambridge
Washington O Salisbury
Harrisonburg O Arlington
Charlottesville O Fredericksburg
Waynesboro O Richmond ●
Petersburg O Newport News
Lynchburg O Norfolk

O Key Cities Served
● Terminal City

Roanoke O McKenney O
Blacksburg O

Winston Salem O ● Raleigh/Durham
Asheville O Greensboro O
Fayetteville O
Charlotte ●
Spartanburg O Wilmington O
Dalton O Greenville ● Florence O
Athens O 1995
Atlanta ● Columbia ●
1995
Augusta O Charleston O

Columbus O

RED ☆ STAR
EXPRESS LINES OF AUBURN INC.

AUBURN   BUFFALO   ROCHESTER   SYRACUSE   NEW YORK CITY
112 CLARK ST.   396 WASHINGTON ST.
PHONE 3111   PHONE WALKER 5-5928

18

RED STAR
☆
PRESS LINES

Thanks to the following for
their help in completing these articles.

Accelerated Transport - Pony Express	David Shields
Benton Express	Herbert Matthews
Bilkay's Express	Bob Kortenhaus
Campbell, H. F. & Sons	Frank Campbell & Jim Morrison
Central Storage & Transfer	Jim Morrison, John Voystock,& Mrs. Mildred Wacker
Eastern Freightways	Mike Shevell & Angie
Horn's Motor Express	David Sheilds
Kingsway Transports LTD	Doug Grieve & T. Brad Dunkin
Lombard Brothers, Inc.	Ronald J. Lombard
Motor Freight Express	Les Wolgemuth
Motor Transport	Edward Schuessler
Oak Harbor Freight Lines	Henry Vander Pol
Riteway Express	Bill Spina
Ruzila's Express	Carol Hagen
System 99	Marvin Gilardi & Ray Mitchell
TNT Red Star Express	Don Rucker

And thanks to my friends for their continued support and   contributions:
John L. Brown, Ed Darrow, T. Brad Dunkin, Mack Foley, Doug
Grieve, Fred Gruin, Jr., J.R. Hodges, Al Koenig, Joseph T. Lincoln,
Russ MacNeil, Gary Morton, Richard Muller, Don Querciagrossa,
Larry Scheef, Bryan Sheehan, Chris Sissick, and Mike Tuttle.

Typesetting - David Stephens
Editing - Don Querciagrossa
Executive Secretary - Sandi Terebecki

THE VANISHING TRUCKING PIONEERS - Sold Out
(213 Pages) Adley Express, Akers Motor Lines, Associated Transport, Brady Motor Frate, Branch, Brown Express, Buckingham, Campbell's 66, Central Motor Lines, Central Truck Lines, D.C. International, Davidson, Dohrn, ET & WNC, East Texas Motor Freight, Garford, Garrett, Gateway, Gordon's, Great Southern, Hennis, Herrin, IML, ICX, Interstate, Johnson, Kramer Bros., LeeWay, LASME, M & M, Mason-Dixon, McLean, Mid-States, Motor Cargo, Navajo, ONC, Pilot, Quinn, RC, Red Arrow, Ringsby, Riss, Smith's, Spector, Super Service, Terminal Transport, T.I.M.E., Wilson Freight $13.95

THE TRUCKING PIONEERS, BOOK II - Still Available
(270 Pages) AAA Trucking, ABF, Admiral Merchants, American Freight, Associated Truck Lines, Briggs, Brown, CW, Carolina, Central Freight Lines, CF, Cooper-Jarrett, Cowan, W.T., Darling, Eastern, Eazor, Fredrickson, Hemingway, Holmes, Inland, Jones, Lyons, Michigan Express, Mushroom, New Dixie, Overnite, P.I.E., Preston, Red Ball, Sanborn's, TIME-DC, Thurston, Transus, Van Brunt, Yellow Freight Systems, Inc. $13.95

THE TRUCKING PIONEERS, BOOK III - Still Available
(210 Pages) All States Freight, Apgar Brothers, Blue Line Express, Boss Linco Lines, Bowman Transportation, Inc., Centralia Cartage, Chippewa Motor Freight, Churchill Truck Lines, Great Lakes Express, Hall's Motor Transit, Keeshin Freight Lines, Mundy Motor Lines, Murphy Motor Freight, P.B. Mutrie Motor Trans., New Penn Motor Express, North Penn Transfer, Novick Transfer Co., Old Dominion Freight Lines, Oneida Motor Freight, Pic-Walsh Freight Co., Ryder Truck Lines, St. Johnsbury Tracking Co, Transamerican Freight Lines, Transcon Lines, Watkins Motor Lines, Watson Wilson Transportation System, H.P. Welch Co., Western Gillette, Wilson Trucking Co., Wooster Express $13.95

THE TRUCKING PIONEERS, BOOK IV -
A & H Truck Line, A-P-A Transport, Allegheny Freight Lines, Arrow Carrier Corp., Bell Lines, Be-Mac Transport Co., Bender & Louden Motor Freight, Chemical-Leaman Tank Lines, Clairmont Transfer Co., Cochrane Transportation Co., Jack Cole Co., Cole's Express, Consolidated Forwarding Co., Cross Transportation, Daniels, Motor Freight, Delta Lines, Dixie-Ohio Express, Frame's Motor Freight, Helm's Express, Johnson Motor Lines, Milne Truck Lines, New England Motor Freight, Olson Transportation Co., Rock Island Motor Transit, Russian Transportation, Saia Motor Freight Line, Shipper's Dispatch, Teal's Express, Yale System $13.95

BOOKS II, III, & IV AVAILABLE :   Pioneer Press
                                    4338 Dover Crossing Drive
                                    Marietta, GA 30066
                                    (770) 591-7300